Land of Bright Promise

The M. K. Brown Range Life Series, No. 17

LAND OF BRIGHT PROMISE

Advertising the Texas Panhandle and South Plains, 1870–1917

By Jan Blodgett

 UNIVERSITY OF TEXAS PRESS   AUSTIN

Copyright © 1988 by the University of Texas Press
All rights reserved
Printed in the United States of America
First edition, 1988
Requests for permission to reproduce material from this work should be sent to:
Permissions
University of Texas Press
Box 7819
Austin, Texas 78713-7819
Library of Congress Cataloging-in-Publication Data
Blodgett, Jan, 1954–
 Land of bright promise: advertising the Texas Panhandle and South Plains,
1870–1917 / by Jan Blodgett. — 1st ed.
  p.   cm. — (The M. K. Brown range life series; no. 17)
 Bibliography: p.
 Includes index.
 1. Land use—Texas—Panhandle—History.   2. Panhandle (Tex.)—
Population—History.   I. Title.   II. Series.
 HD266.T42P362 1988
 333.73′15′097648—dc 19   87-2531
 ISBN 978-0-292-74223-9   CIP

Publication of this work has been made possible in part by a grant from the
Andrew W. Mellon Foundation.

*To all the teachers who have been friends
and all the friends who have been teachers*

Contents

Illustrations

Acknowledgments

A FAVORITE question that is posed to every newcomer to the Panhandle–South Plains of Texas is "Why did you choose to come
here?" Although invariably proud of the area, local residents generally seem surprised that anyone else would come here to live. In
fact, not until the turn of the twentieth century did many people
express any interest in this area. I would like to thank all those who
helped in this study of how settlers were attracted to the Plains.

This book could not have been written without the unfailing
support of family and friends. The staff at the Panhandle-Plains
Historical Museum and the members of the history faculty at West
Texas State University helped with the many resources available
there, as did my former co-workers at the Cornette Library at West
Texas State University. To my co-workers at the Southwest Collection, Texas Tech University, friends who provided housing, and my
father, who provided extra typing, I owe a special debt of gratitude
for all the assistance, encouragement, and patience.

Finally, I would like to recognize all those pioneers and boosters
who left records as to why they chose the Panhandle–South Plains
of Texas as home.

Land of Bright Promise

I.

Introduction

THE FINAL stage of permanent settlement for the Panhandle–South Plains of Texas was marked by the arrival of farmers and the development of agriculture as a major industry. The Panhandle–South Plains became a center of activity for land agents and colonizers around the turn of the twentieth century. During the years from 1890 through 1917, this area changed from the domain of ranchers and their cattle to a promised land for farmers and their families. For example, by 1890 changes in the cattle industry and an increased demand for farmlands convinced the owners of the vast XIT Ranch that the time had finally come to open up 80,000 acres of their holdings to colonization by farmers.[1]

However, by that time several myths and images had taken hold in the public imagination, and these concepts would challenge all future advertisers of the region. Indeed, for almost sixty years prior to the turn of the century government reports, travel journals, textbooks, and articles and illustrations in popular magazines, newspapers, and novels introduced and developed images of the Plains area as a desert, as a haven for desperate characters, as the private domain of ranchers or Indians, but rarely as a future agricultural wonderland.

This wide selection of publications indicated a strong interest on the part of the American public about the area. Americans have long been noted for their interest in themselves and their country. Even those on the frontier maintained a strong interest in other new areas. A study by Howard Peckham of libraries and library use in frontier Ohio has revealed that most towns, regardless of size or age, had established libraries and that these libraries and their organizers betrayed "a noticeable weakness for books of travel and

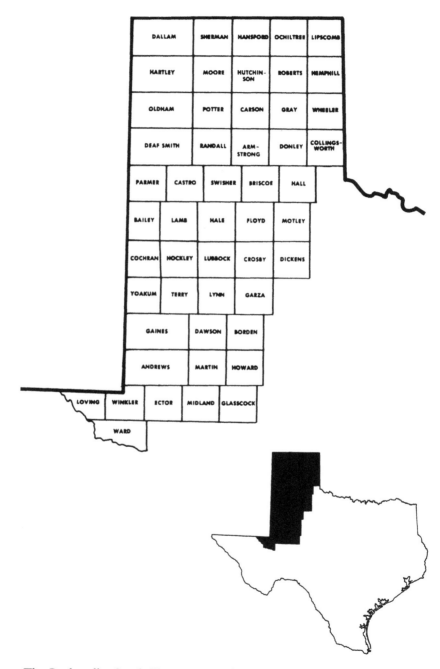

The Panhandle–South Plains region of Texas.

description. We might think that in opening new countries themselves, they would have fulfilled their dreams and satisfied their urge
for learning about distant places." Peckham also notes that "they
seemed eager to read about Lewis and Clark, Zebulon Pike and
Jonathan Carver, as well as about the Holy Land, Europe and Asia.
Possibly they gloried in making comparisons with their own
vistas."[2]

Spanish explorers published the first reports about the Panhandle–South Plains area, but these reports had little impact, especially for Anglo-Americans.[3] The first accounts to capture the
imagination of the American public were those of government explorers, including Lewis and Clark, Zebulon Pike, and Stephen
Long. However, the work of these explorers was not aimed at encouraging settlement but rather at finding routes to the Pacific or
across the Rocky Mountains. As such, the tendency was to portray
the area as being "an obstacle blocking the path of the explorer
intent on what lay beyond."[4]

One result of this attitude was the introduction of the idea of the
Plains as a desert. The Long Expedition of 1819 gave official sanc-
tion to the expression "Great American Desert." Although Long's
description of the area did not contain any new insights, his report
did include a map with the legend "Great American Desert" written across the Plains area.[5] The impact of this map was such that,
by 1822 and for the next half-century, map publishers and cartographers readily copied the map and the term. As new maps were
issued, the area defined as desert grew far beyond Long's original
limits. As Frederic Paxon noted, "School boys of the thirties, for-
ties, and fifties were told that from the bend in the Missouri to the
Stony Mountains stretched an American desert." These school
texts further embellished this image with maps colored "brown with
the speckled aspect that connotes Sahara or Arabia, with camels,
oases, and sand dunes."[6]

Martin Bowden has identified 184 such geographies and textbooks, most of which were intended for "colleges, academics, sec-
ondary schools, and the well-educated" rather than as elementary
texts. These books generally were limited in distribution to the
northeastern states.[7] Less limited in audience were the atlases such
as *The Woodbridge and Willard Geography of 1824*, *The Carey and Lee
Atlas of 1827*, and T. G. Bradford's *Comprehensive Atlas of 1835*, all
of which contained variations on the desert theme.[8]

Just as cartographers unquestioningly accepted the Great American Desert label of the Long report, so the desert description went
unchallenged by the efforts of later government explorers such as

Lieutenant James Abert, Captain Randolph Marcy, and First Lieutenant Amiel Whipple. Indeed, in 1854 the U.S. Boundary Commission issued a map with this description of the Llano Estacado: "The Whole country from the head waters of the Red, Brazos and Colorado rivers to the Rio Pecos is a sterile and barren plain without water or timber producing only a few stunted shrubs which are insufficient to sustain animal life."[9] The continued acceptance of the Plains as a desert caused some speculation that the government was interested in maintaining the myth as a politically safe solution to the Indian problem or even the slavery issue. John Tice, a member of the Missouri State Board of Agriculture, charged in his 1872 *Annual Report* that the desert myth had been used to reconcile the extreme Southerners to the Missouri Compromise by convincing them that the territory, although free, was worthless.[10] John C. Calhoun and the War Department were singled out by Tice as early perpetuators of the myth.

The War Department was actually only one of several government agencies involved in issuing reports about the area, and Tice's comments were soon overshadowed by a far greater controversy. By the 1840s the demand for land began to clash with the notion of the desert, and the public discovered the ideas of John C. Fremont, William Gilpin, and Thomas Hart Benton, who were redefining the Plains as a great meadow or pastoral domain.[11] The idea of the Plains as pastureland soon gave way to the joint myths of "the garden in the grassland" and "rain follows the plow," especially in Kansas and Nebraska. The debate over increased rainfall, while not directly tied to the Texas Plains, had important implications for land-selling techniques there.

The desire to find a way to make these lands into the new garden area of the nation fueled the efforts of rainmakers. As the debate about increased rainfall grew, government agencies were besieged by those seeking to prove their theories. In 1890 the Division of Forestry of the U.S. Department of Agriculture received an additional $2,000 in appropriations for rainmaking experiments. The next year responsibility for the experiments shifted to the assistant secretary of agriculture, and additional appropriations were made in 1891 and 1892.[12] The Weather Bureau, while not actively involved with the rainmaking schemes, handled numerous letters from would-be rainmakers as did the governors and agriculture departments of the states of Kansas, Colorado, and Nebraska.[13] Arguments and counterarguments were published in both state and federal government reports, in House and Senate journals, and in the scientific and popular journals of the time.[14] Government officials often included the reports of individuals in their official reports and responded to other theories in popular publications. One of the strongest opponents to the increased-rainfall theories was geologist John Wesley Powell. Powell's *Report on the Lands of the Arid Region of the United States, with a More Detailed Account of the Lands of Utah* was popular enough to require a second printing, but his recommendations found strong opposition. [15]

Government officials soon recognized the educational value of their reports, and in 1895 the secretary of the Department of Agriculture was charged with preparing an annual report that was to include "such reports from the different bureaus and divisions and such papers prepared by their special agents, accompanied by suitable illustrations, as shall, in the opinion of the Secretary, be specially suited to interest and instruct the farmers of the country." [16] In the following years the annual reports of the secretary included such articles as "The Weather Bureau and the Homemaker" (1905), "Successful Wheat Growing in Semiarid Districts" (1901), "Diversified Farming in the Cotton Belt: Texas" (1906), "The So-Called Change of Climate in the Semiarid West" (1909), "Farming as an Occupation for City-bred Men" (1910), "The Water Economy of Dry Land Crops" (1912), and "Some Misconceptions Concerning Dry-Farming" (1912).

Although the Agriculture Department of the State of Texas had also begun publishing reports earlier, the value of the Panhandle area was not acknowledged until 1910. As noted by Commissioner of Agriculture Edward Kone in his introduction to the first bulletin issued about the Panhandle:

> The Texas Department of Agriculture has had an increasing demand for information about the Plains and Panhandle of Texas. The data at the command of the Department for furnishing those interested the desired information, have been so meagre and scattered that the Department was not satisfied with the service it was rendering to a large and important region of Texas. . . . This territory being largely an undeveloped one to which there is an almost unprecedented tide of immigration, it was my further purpose to secure data as to crops and methods of cultivation, as well, as live stock and methods of grazing and feeding, as would be an elementary guide for the "new settler." [17]

This bulletin, written by Frederick Mally, described approximately forty crops and their suitability for the Panhandle and Llano Estacado area along with suggestions for livestock raising. The report was cautious in tone and acknowledged that at least one five-county area "will ever be the great pasture of the Panhandle."[18] This work reflected the sense of responsibility expected of government documents, a sense of responsibility that was occasionally lacking in the other types of materials available to the reading public.

Particularly notorious for inaccuracies but still very popular reading were the travelogues and journals. Since they were recorded as personal observations, they did not have to answer to accuracy. That they were not always the reports of disinterested parties can be seen in the disclaimers that appeared in later journals. L. P. Brockett in *Our Western Empire*, published in 1881, protested:

> To all such inquirers, we propose to give the information which they seek and we beg leave to assure them at the start, that we have no object in view, except their benefit. We have no interest in any railroad, land grant, colony, mining, farming, stock raising, or wool-growing company or organization west of the Mississippi river, we do not own a square foot of land west of that river, and do not expect to do so; but we know the country, its advantages and disadvantages, and we propose to state these honestly and fairly. We could obtain the endorsement of all the governors, senators, and representatives of that entire region, to the truthfulness and fairness of our book, if it were needful; but we think that every one who will read it will be satisfied for themselves that it is an honest and trustworthy book.[19]

Brockett included descriptions of the Panhandle and Llano Estacado areas, and while his analysis of the benefits of mesquite is questionable, he did not dodge the issue of the water supply. His comments about the area include the following statement:

> Where these lands are broken up and plowed deeply, the roots of the mezquite aid in bringing up the moisture from below, and the rainfall increases from year to year. Eventually all these alkaline lands, or nearly all, will be brought under cultivation, and will prove either with or without irrigation, some of the most productive and valuable lands of the West. . . . it [the Panhandle] is not well watered, and sections of it are not watered at all except by wells. Its rainfall is very small, and the pasturage, though scanty, is nutritious where water can be obtained.[20]

J. H. Beadle was less kind in *The Undeveloped West*. Published almost a decade earlier than Brockett's work, *The Undeveloped West* identified the desert area of the Plains as encompassing over one million square miles of "a region of varying mountain, desert and rock, of prevailing drought or complete sterility, broken rarely by fertile valleys; of dead volcanoes and sandy wastes; of excessive chemicals, dust, gravel and other inorganic matter."[21] Beadle's assessment echoed that of Josiah Gregg, who provided one of the first nongovernmental reports about this area. Gregg limited his Great Western Prairies to 400,000 square miles but found them equally inhospitable. In his work *Commerce of the Prairies*, published in 1844, he noted that this region is chiefly uninhabitable:

> not so much for want of wood (though the plains are altogether naked), as of soil and water; for though some of the plains appear of sufficiently fertile soil, they are mostly of a sterile character, and all too dry to be cultivated. These great steppes seem only fitted for the haunts of the mustangs, the buffalo, the antelope, and their migratory lord, the prairie Indian. Unless with the progressive influence of time, some favorable mutation should be wrought in nature's operations, to revive the plains and upland prairies, the occasional fertile valleys are too isolated and remote to become the abodes of civilized man.[22]

At the other end of the spectrum was Richard Elliott's *Notes Taken in Sixty Years*. Elliott was an active proponent of increased rainfall and the importance of railroads in opening the West. He was, in fact, employed by the Kansas Pacific Railway as an "industrial agent." Elliott modestly described the creation of his position: "It meant, that I must be in some a geologist, a botanist, a farmer, a meteorologist, a horticulturalist and a philosopher general . . . to test by experiment the capabilities of the country." He further stressed, "If I should fail in proving the wealth of the country, I could at least demonstrate that it had a railway in it. No such mission had ever been undertaken before or probably ever will be again."[23]

Even as Elliott overstated his case for increased rainfall, so he made his position more novel than it was. Railroads had a vested interest in increasing public awareness of their lines and the lands they crossed and were among the most active promoters of new farmlands. Indeed, travel journals were often published with the silent backing of the railroads. Author Robert Strahorn received the support of the Union Pacific with the admonition to make his book *To the Rockies and Beyond* "anonymous and original."[24]

These travel journals introduced a second myth about the area, that of the "Wild West." While many writers used their travel books to expound on desert and rainfall theories, others built an image that has outlasted even that of the desert. The terrors of the desert paled in comparison to those of renegade Indians and outlaws. In his study of tourism in the West Earl Pomeroy has noted that "as late as 1881, the threat of raids in the Southwest led the Santa Fe Railway to provide trains with Winchester rifles, and passengers to feel that they were re-enacting and equaling the perils of the pioneer wagon crossings."[25] While the Panhandle area was not included in many tourist jaunts,[26] it did begin to figure in fictional tales of fearful Indians and desperadoes. Typical of these novels and short stories were *The Throwback* by Alfred Henry Lewis, *The White Chief* by Captain Mayne Reid, and *The Dead Horseman* by Frederick Holbrook. In these works the Panhandle served as a bleak background for tales of dark deeds and wild cowboys.[27] Just as the authors of travel guides reporting deserts found support in government reports, the tellers of the Wild West myth found support in the works of novelists and artists. These writers and artists played an important role in defining the West. As Sanford Marovitz has stated, "Eastern authors were creating a cultural bridge that would bring readers back home an image of the actual West even as the writers of fiction brought it to life with color, hyperbole, and melodrama. The result was an inevitable mix of romance and realism . . ."[28]

The novelists and artists often brought with them many prejudices and preconceived notions of the West and what it should be. Most of the early stories were written by easterners, not all of whom verified their details by visiting the area.[29] Some of the works produced about the West became classics, such as Washington Irving's *Tour of the Prairies* (1855), Helen Hunt Jackson's *Ramona* (1884), the stories of Bret Harte and Mark Twain, Owen Wister's *The Virginian* (1902), and Zane Grey's *Riders of the Purple Sage* (1912). Public interest in western fiction supported not only these authors but dozens of lesser talents. Eramus Beadle launched his dime-novel series in 1860, with the original series consisting of 300 tales. In the next three decades thousands of similar tales appeared.[30] Both Texas and the Great Plains were popular settings for these tales and soon acquired the image of lands that could never be conquered, lands without a place for farmers. As Henry Nash Smith has explained in *Virgin Land*, "Even if American frontiersmen should push out upon the plains, and take up the pastoral life imposed upon them by the environment, they would become nomadic brigands, a menace to settled agricultural communities farther to the East."[31]

The civilizing influence of agriculture did not appear in popular fiction until the turn of the century with the development of realistic farm-life fiction beginning around 1910.[32] These novels were in direct contrast with the escapist lore of the dime novels. Writers such as Edgar Watson Howe and Hamlin Garland told grim tales of hardship, loneliness, and economic woes. These novels might have produced a stronger legacy for land sellers to combat had they appeared any earlier. As it was, the more romantic images captured the public imagination and haunted the land agents.

Artists also contributed their visions of the new frontier, visions that were often imbued with strong prejudices.[33] They began recording their impressions of the West along with those of the early explorers and continued to produce works independent of and in conjunction with written accounts. George Catlin, Alfred Jacob Miller, Albert Bierstadt, Thomas Moran, Frederic Remington, and Charles Marion Russell all added to the splendor and mythology pertaining to the West.[34] The images of these and other artists often reached the reading public as illustrations in novels or in the ever-popular monthly magazines. These magazines, such as *Harper's Weekly* and *Frank Leslie's Illustrated Newspaper*, often sent special artists to record impressions of the West for their readers.[35] At least one western artist found himself in conflict with the demands of eastern editors. Maynard Dixon, a popular illustrator, explained his frustrations in a letter to publisher Charles Lummis. He wrote, "I am being paid to lie about the West. I'm going back home where I can do honest work."[36]

Magazines were another important source of information for would-be settlers, providing both factual and fictional accounts of Texas and the Plains area for their readers. These articles served to maintain interest in both the area and the myths about the area. Ray Stannard Baker made this astute observation in the May 1902 issue of *Century Magazine*:

> No other part of the United States is less generally well known than the Southwest, and none is better worth knowing. Of no other part of the United States is so large a portion of the unpleasant and unattractive features known so well, and so small a proportion of the beauties, wonders, and utilities known so little. To the Eastern and Northern mind the Southwest

raises a dim picture of hot desert, bare mountain, and monotonous plain sparsely grown up to cactus, sage, greasewood, or bunch-grass, and sown with white bones of animals which have perished from hunger and thirst; a land of wild Indians, of lazy Mexicans, of rough cowboys, of roving, half-wild cattle, of desperate mining ventures, of frequent train robberies. This impression is based in part on the stray paragraphs from this unknown land that occasionally creep into the metropolitan newspapers, but it is chiefly founded on the hasty observations and reports of dusty, transcontinental travelers, car-weary for three or four days, the edge of interest quite blunted with longing for the green wonders and soft sunshine of California.[37]

Presenting his view of the beauties, the wonders, and the coming of civilization in a two-part series, Baker assured his readers that "a celebrating cowboy or miner sometimes breaks loose and shoots or a Mexican uses a knife, but without the old spirit of the game. Killing has grown distinctly unpopular."[38]

Three years later William Draper was heralding the passing of the cowboy and large ranches,[39] and yet seven years later *The Independent* became a forum for a debate on six-shooter ethics, with a native Texan declaring that certain occasions still warranted settling by violence and an eastern editor decrying this brand of "Texan ethics."[40] Other writers provided insight and opinions on Texas history, politics, health concerns, education, and economy.

Besides information of a general nature about Texas, magazine readers were offered more specific information about agricultural possibilities and techniques. Articles on dry-land farming and irrigation were not limited to agriculture magazines and often appeared on the pages of *The Nation, Harper's New Monthly Magazine, The American Monthly Review of Reviews, Gunton's Magazine,* and *National Geographic.* The myth of the Great American Desert held strong in early publications and remained a theme in later articles. While hardly considered good publicity, these articles did help to inform settlers of the need for new farming techniques for the area.

Opinions on the agricultural possibilities of the area varied as widely as those on social conditions and personal safety, and each aspect was important to future settlers. An agricultural wonderland inhabited by desperate characters was no wonderland, while the best schools and society were of little value in barren lands. The future settlers of the Panhandle–South Plains were interested more in financial stability than in conquering new lands. As Robert Athearn has noted in his study of the Great Plains, "The average newcomer was no broadaxe and long-rifle man, he was a transplanted farmer, and he wanted no more than to pursue his profession . . . These were people who believed what they had read, weighed the apparent advantages of a new opportunity against the disadvantages of their present condition, and signed up for a trip to the promised land."[41]

The land agents in the Panhandle area deliberately sought out farmers and skilled laborers who would be permanent settlers. In order to attract such people, land agents and boosters had not only to praise their lands but also to counter the negative images of deserts, wild Indians, outlaws, powerful ranchers, dangerous cowboys, and lonely stretches of uncivilized plains. Given authority by government reports, life and color by novelists and illustrators, and popularity by magazines and newspapers, these images provided a very real concern for land agents. While the agents were aided by land hunger and rising land prices in the midwestern farming areas, attracting settlers to the Plains required determination and a strong faith in the land itself. Those who successfully brought people to the Plains shared this faith. They were committed to bringing only those who could and would stay in the Panhandle or South Plains. This commitment can be seen in their advertisements and their efforts to help settlers after the land sales had been made.

2.

The Boosters

EVEN DURING the bonanza years of the cattle industry, there was interest in bringing new settlers to the Texas Panhandle and South Plains. Residents of the small communities that had sprung up before the 1890s quickly developed a sense of civic pride and boosterism. Indeed, the desire to induce others to come to a new home was a striking characteristic of these settlers. William Curry Holden observed that "no sooner had sufficient people arrived to organize a county, than they began to take steps to encourage other people to come. They wanted neighbors, they craved the things which are made possible by community life such as social affairs, schools and churches."[1] These early settlers also craved the economic stability that additional population would bring.

Cattlemen and investors in ranching operations were slower to acknowledge the benefits of an increased population, especially one of farmers, but after 1890 many joined in the design to populate the plains. More settlers meant higher land values, increased trade, and a greater need for services and businesses. While the landowners and investors stood to make the most direct profits, several other groups willingly led the boosterism and promotion of immigration of this area. These boosters varied from one section of the area to another but basically fall into five categories: local newspaper editors, commercial clubs and immigration societies, railroads, real estate agents and speculators, and landowners.[2]

While each of these groups sought new settlers for their own reasons, they were united in the desire for an increased and stable population. This was especially true for those whose profits would come indirectly—the newspaper editors and commercial club members. For these, land sales alone would not necessarily bring new customers for their businesses and longevity for their communities. They sought land buyers who would be permanent and prosperous citizens and searched for settlers to share their dreams, to enhance their prosperity, and to prove their hopes possible. This combination of potential gain and idealism gave rise to their booster efforts and yet led to some seeming contradictions. While each town rivaled its neighbor, the competition did not preclude cooperative efforts with neighboring towns where campaigns were often carried on simultaneously. And while the boosters designed campaigns to attract only those identified as acceptable citizens, in their enthusiasm they often failed to limit their claims and adjectives.

This enthusiasm is most evident in the work of the local newspaper editors. Maintaining a pattern established by earlier frontier editors, these men and women considered themselves to be above any suspicion of vested interest and working solely for the benefit of their chosen community.[3] If their community had not quite earned all the adjectives applied to it, belief that it soon would was ample justification. In describing the efforts of editors, Daniel Boorstin has noted, "History will never tell how diligently the editors sought for facts to influence homeseekers, and how enthusiastically close they often came to bearing false witness, not against their neighbors, but in behalf of them." After all, editors could defend their actions in believing that "It was permissible to mix visions and prophecies with current and negotiable realities when it was certain to come true."[4]

Clarendon's *Northwest Texas*, the first recorded newspaper in the Texas Panhandle, appeared in 1878 shortly after the founding of the town. Thereafter, few communities were ever established in the area without a newspaper office also being established. According to E. R. Archambeau, the prerequisites for starting a paper during this period were "a 'shirt-tail' full of type, a simple handpress, an editor with a large amount of courage and a dedication and determination to help develop his adopted community into the 'Metropolis of the Plains' or the 'Paradise of the Panhandle.'"[5]

The activities of these early editors were noted on the pages of the *Tascosa Pioneer*, where the area's newspaper industry was monitored. On Saturday, 19 November 1887, *The Pioneer*'s editor reported: "*The Crescent*, published at Canadian, is the tenth Panhandle newspaper. Eighteen months ago *The Pioneer* came into the field, number three. Eight have started since, one of them after a brief struggle giving it up. Some of the ten are evidently on terra firma, and nearly all are coming to something like an idea of the size and nature of their work, Great is the Panhandle." By 1891 *The Pioneer* had "given it up" and the editor, C. F. Rudolph, had moved to the *Channing Register.* [6]

The failure of a newspaper rarely dampened the enthusiasm of editors; their efforts at promotion were simply continued in earnest at a new location. Among the most active newspapers in the Texas Panhandle and South Plains were the Canyon City papers, the *Hereford Brand*, the *Dalhart Texan*, the *Crosbyton Review*, the *Hale County Herald*, and the *Daily Panhandle.* Other area papers such as the Amarillo papers and the *Lubbock Avalanche* shared in the boosterism, with the level of activity varying as communities became more established and as outside interest focused on various sections of the area. Those papers remaining solvent during all of the boom years reflect well the changes in their communities, the hopes achieved, and the plans lost. Editors were limited only by their imaginations and occasionally their awareness of civic responsibility.

The first editor of the Canyon City (later Canyon) newspaper *The Stayer* expressed definite reservations about boomers in a 1902 editorial, stating: "*The Stayer* has never boomed this country and never expects to. There is a large floating population in the farming sections of Texas and the Territories that is constantly shifting about, always seeking the Utopia they would not stay in if they found. This class happily has not seen fit to invade the Plains and we hope they never will. . . . We hope to see the Plains country yet settled with stock farmers, each owning his own home, a bunch of good cattle and keeping them in good order on home raised feed." [7]

The emphasis of this paper quickly shifted from livestock to agriculture with the advent of George Brandon as the new editor in 1903. During his tenure the editorials of the renamed *Canyon City News* stressed the need for "more farmers, more farms and better farming." [8] The *Hereford Brand* began active boosting several years before the Canyon City papers and along with the *Hale County Herald* encouraged the early attempts at irrigation as part of the transition to agriculture.

Unlike many of the other area towns, Crosbyton did not witness the shift from cattle to agriculture. The community was founded in 1908 as part of a land promotion venture and the boosterism of its newspaper exactly matched the nature of the little town. The *Crosbyton Review* was one of the leading advertisers of the Plains, offering support to almost any effort to promote immigration. This enthusiasm rarely flagged; as late as the summer of 1916, the paper was featuring full-page ads for the town's "Prosperity Carnival" and articles urging citizens to resolve:

That you'll keep so busy boosting that you won't have any time to knock. That you'll vote, talk and work for a bigger, better and brighter town. . . . That you'll say something good about this town every time you write a letter. . . . That you'll brag about this town so much that you'll have to work for this town in order to keep from being a liar. . . . That you'll make friends with the farmers, if a town man, or with town folks, if a farmer, and help work together for the good of the community of which this town is the center.[9]

However, by this same time, other area papers had begun to shift away from booster efforts. The *Hereford Brand* included more national news, and editorials stressed civic improvements, while the *Randall County News* emphasized local activities and state politics. Interest in promotions was still evident in the Panhandle State Fair edition of the *News*, issued on 7 September 1916, but the glowing adjectives were giving way to practical thought. In a 1917 editorial discussing the implications of a false story about neighboring Hereford's rate of housing construction, a cautious note was sounded: "No Panhandle town needs to lie about it[s] exact condition. All of the towns are growing and if they are not building a hundred or even fifty houses a season, it is because they do not need them. It is better to grow as there is need for growth than to spurt out with a big quantity of houses and have them vacant."[10]

The promotional activities of these newspapers included publishing editorials and articles encouraging immigration; issuing special editions; producing extra copies for out-of-state distribution; serving as an advertising medium for land agents and companies; and cooperating with the publication of promotional leaflets and magazines. Daniel Boorstin has characterized these newspapers and activities as "probably our earliest media of national advertising."[11]

Well aware that their audiences went far beyond current town limits, editors addressed articles and editorials to both local citizens and future settlers. Current citizens were educated about the possibilities of the area, while others were invited to join them. The banners or mottoes printed beneath the names of the newspapers often reflected the editors' boomer intentions. The early issues of the *Hereford Brand* proclaimed it "A Weekly Paper Devoted to the Interest of the Panhandle of Texas," while the *Canyon City News* requested, "If You Are a Panhandler, Help the News 'Panhandle' for the Panhandle of Texas." And the *Crosbyton Review* called itself "A Newspaper For The Whole People Of The South Plains Of Texas." Other banners appealed directly to new settlers in stating, "A Very Good Investment—A Home In Randall County" or "Plainview's Slogan: Nothing Shallow But The Water." [12]

Articles and editorials displayed a wide range of promotional interest. In some cases the distinction between the two blurred with more than a little editorializing appearing in front-page articles. Articles varied from straightforward accounts of farming activities to educational tracts on farming methods to glowing descriptions of town development. Typical *Randall County News* headlines included "Warm Days Make Wheat Grow Fast," "Alfalfa Is Coming Out in Splendid Condition," "Apple Most Hardy Fruit—Plains Country Best Place in the World for Its Culture," and "Broom Corn Makes Farmer Big Money." The *Crosbyton Review* added articles on "First Train Over Crosbyton—Southplains R.R.," "Crosbyton Over-Run with Prospectors," and "Crop Conditions Fine in Crosbyton Country Idlelands." The *Dalhart Texan* kept readers informed of the activities of local land agencies, while the *Hale County Herald* reported on the arrival of new settlers. In addition to articles on these topics, space was found for photographs, rainfall charts, and even poetry to illustrate the prosperity and potential of the area. One poem, reprinted in the *Hereford Brand*, managed to include references to the climate, water, rainfall, crops, and the public school fund. [13]

Special columns and correspondence provided further opportunities for boomer articles. The *Crosbyton Review* responded to a query about the role of women in the development of the Plains by introducing a "Woman's Corner," and later announced that "we have made arrangements for a school correspondent and will keep our readers in touch with what the school is doing all the time for the full term." [14] Other newspapers not only used special correspondents but also reprinted articles from neighboring papers and accepted articles written by land company officials and railroad agents. The *Hale County Herald* published articles carrying a Texas Land and Development Company by-line. Educational in nature, the articles discussed good farming methods, including irrigation, and urged settlers to try them. [15] The *Hereford Brand* and *Randall County News* regularly carried articles written by Professor H. M. Bainer, Santa Fe Railroad's agricultural agent, which were also educational and stressed scientific farming principles. Articles reprinted from other newspapers were usually more descriptive than educational, perhaps offered to prove that the editor's opinions were shared by others. The *Canyon City News* reproduced editorials from both the *Quanah Tribune-Chief* and the *Hale Center Messenger* calling for cooperation and assistance in advertising the Plains. The editor of the *Daily Panhandle* found a favorable article in the Kansas City *Drovers Telegraph* and reprinted it in full for his readers, while his counterpart at the *Lubbock Avalanche* borrowed excerpts from a railroad journal to assure readers that the Great American Desert was a hoax.[16] These editors were also quick to criticize any unflattering reports and correct any misrepresentations. The *Daily Panhandle* of 18 January 1911 featured the editorial "Panhandle Slandered Again," which decried the unfair coverage of recent winter weather by "many eastern papers."

Editorials were not always confined to the editorial page, and while not limited to booster topics, they did often deal with promotional efforts. Just as many of the articles were really intended for eastern and midwestern readers, the editorials were designed for a range of audiences and purposes. Some editorials were educational, supporting new farming techniques or particular crops, while others were purely promotional, and still others were inspirational, urging community support and civic pride.

Editors were quick to note their own efforts even as they were encouraging their readers to take an active part in promotion. Readers were assured that newspapers and, in turn, advertisements in newspapers were vital promotional tools. While encouraging local businesses to purchase advertising, many newspapers ran their own advertisements for the town. The *Crosby County News* carried a series of ads on "Crosby County's New Baby," and the *West Texas News* placed half-page notices announcing, "Wanted at once 1000 families." These notices offered the unusual plan of having families come in to help gather the harvest and then stay on as permanent residents of Scurry County.[17]

George Brandon of the *Canyon City News* was a strong advocate of advertising and often assured his readers of its importance. In an early editorial, he wrote, "Mind you, the only foreign representative or advertisement for a town is her local paper, unless that town has progressed to the extent of having advertising committees or immigration bureaus. A practical and successful business man in seeking a new location can determine at one glance at the local paper if that town is worthy of his attention and investment, and it is invariably the case that this fact is the deciding point in making the selection of the town."[18] Reviving this theme, Brandon later lavished praise upon the citizens of Hereford and the *Hereford Brand*:

> Among newspapermen Hereford has the name of being the best newspaper town in Northwest Texas. . . . To its newspapers, particularly the *Brand*, Hereford and Deaf Smith County in the opinion of *The News*, owes for the gain in actual settlers over other Plains counties during the past two years. The papers land them and the country does the rest. As a town Hereford is not better situated than many other Plains towns and not nearly so well in a natural sense as is Canyon City. And, as a county Deaf Smith is, not any better if as good as other Plains counties, but not withstanding all this they, both town and county are leading the gain in settlers. There are other things, of course, aside from this advantage, but where a country is judged by its newspapers, and nine out of ten adopt this very course, the credit should be given where it belongs—to the newspapers.[19]

To offer his readers every opportunity to equal the efforts of Hereford and Deaf Smith County, Brandon instituted a special subscription rate for papers sent out of state. F. E. White, editor of the *Crosbyton Review*, was forced to introduce a charge for extra copies of his paper after finding the burden of free distribution too heavy. On the South Plains the *Crosby County News* pioneered newspaper boosterism by printing several hundred extra copies of each edition for mailing to all parts of the United States.[20] White also adopted this practice with his Crosbyton paper, but when no longer able to continue he explained to his readers:

> The Review management have from the first issue of the Review, on Jan. 14th, 1909 to April 13th, 1911, given away an average of 222 copies of the Review each week, making 119 weeks, the total of which is 24,198 copies, and at 5 cents per copy would be the nice sum of $1,209.90. . . . If you have a bunch of people you would like to see the Review, have their name placed on the list or hand in a nickle each and have a sample copy sent them. When you support an enterprise with a little filthy lucre, you feel better toward it any way . . . we ask those who are interested in the county, town and the developments of the same to do your part and lets keep the Review going to many new people each week. We can do this if you will come across, but we cannot do it alone.[21]

White not only encouraged his readers to buy extra copies, he also took time to assure them that they were actually eager to do so. In an editorial on November 10, 1910, he congratulated them on their interest in a special edition and reported that "we have received orders for copies of the edition as soon as off the press from seven different states and in numbers from ten to sixty." The out-of-state interest was in addition to the many local citizens who "wanted copies of the special and gave us other encouragement."

Special editions were very much a part of the newspaper booster tradition. Occasionally they would be issued in conjunction with a local event, but for most editors no special excuse was needed. Usually featuring stories on each of the towns' businesses, these special editions also contained numerous photographs of fine homes, public buildings, farms, and fields of crops. Also popular were articles describing the town's phenomenal growth in recent years and its certain future.[22] The *Crosbyton Review* editor had few equals in presenting his town's present and future. The headlines for the *Review*'s first special edition announced:

THE EYES OF THE WORLD ARE TURNED TOWARD THE SOUTH PLAINS. CROSBYTON, THE CITY OF DESTINY, IS THEIR MECCA.

Not a city that's going to be, but, a city that is—Something about the things we have in sight—Something about the people who are responsible for Crosbyton's existance—And who are and have been responsible for the great things that have come to a city with a future—Watch Crosbyton.[23]

Two years later the headline for another special edition read, "Crosbyton, Texas in 1920. The Fastest Growing Town in the State—Come and See." Underneath this banner was a "photo" (actually a sketch made to look like a photograph) displaying a Crosbyton of tree-lined boulevards, many-storied businesses, and a stately, domed courthouse building dominating the public square.[24] The feature story for this edition consisted of letters written to the editor from individuals affiliated with the CB Livestock Company detailing the company's future plans for the little town and reminding readers of the company's past efforts.

Other special or booster editions of area newspapers also featured letters or testimonials from farmers and businessmen recounting their successes and reasons for moving to the particular town or county. A special promotional magazine, the *Texas Panhandle Magazine*, consisted almost entirely of reprints of such letters. This journal received considerable support from the area's newspapers and even borrowed articles and photographs from them.[25]

Another important aspect of these special editions, and newspaper promotion in general, was advertising by local businesses. Letters describing agricultural success certainly helped fill out booster editions, but the advertisements helped to pay for them. Editors occasionally felt compelled to remind local businessmen of the important impact of the paper in its role of "foreign representative" and of the need to support the paper and its work. One such editorial in the *Canyon News* was directed to real estate agents in particular. The editor explained that he had received two letters asking why local land agents did not advertise in the paper. He included excerpts from these letters and concluded the column by directing the question to the nonadvertisers.[26]

One reason for the initial lack of advertisements was that the boosterism of the newspapers actually preceded the existence of real estate firms by a number of years. The newspaper's function of serving as an advertising medium for real estate agents and land companies did not develop until immigration began on a significant scale. Land offices then opened their doors and started advertising campaigns, often relying heavily upon newspapers. The *Randall County News* and the *Crosbyton Review* had particularly close ties with local real estate firms, the Keiser Brothers and Phillips Land Company and the CB Livestock Company respectively. The *Crosbyton Review* not only carried extensive advertising for the CB Livestock Company but also printed numerous articles and editorials praising the efforts of the company and its vice-president, Julian Bassett.[27] Newspaper offices often printed brochures for real estate companies and, in the case of the 10 November 1905 issue of the *Canyon City News*, shared photographs. In that issue the *News* featured two pages of photographs lent by the Canyon City Real Estate Company.

The eagerness of newspaper editors to share and cooperate with local businesses extended beyond encouraging the purchase of advertising space. They also actively supported the organization and development of commercial clubs and chambers of commerce. As noted by Canyon's George Brandon, few towns could support special advertising committees or immigration bureaus in the early years of their development. However, once sufficient support was available, the formation of a commercial club or board of trade was inevitable. The enthusiasm of these groups often matched that of the newspaper editors, who were frequently active members.[28] Usually comprised of the area's leading businessmen as well as farmers and ranchers, these organizations took the lead in establishing railroad connections and planning civic improvements. The goals of the Hereford Commercial Club in 1910 as identified by D. M. Lynch were:

> trains in operation on a north-south railroad, free mail delivery, an effort to make Hereford a health resort attracting one thousand summer visitors, a first class hotel, paving, public parks, a causeway across Tierra Blanca Creek, completion of the high school and courthouse, one hundred thousand trees planted in and around town, five hundred houses built in the town and occupied by two thousand progressive people, five hundred new farms opened and operated by industrious, scientific farmers, a flour mill and a fire company organized and equipped.[29]

Even with such elaborate designs, interest in commercial clubs and boards fluctuated, with many of these clubs undergoing periodic reorganizations or revivals. The first Commercial Club in Lubbock was organized in August 1907 with approximately sixty members. It underwent reorganization in late 1908 or early 1909 and then disbanded in 1910. The Chamber of Commerce, established in 1913, finally proved to be a stable and important source of boosterism for the community. Similarly, the first meeting of the Crosbyton Commercial Club was announced in the 14 January 1909 issue of the *Review*, and four months later attempts were still being made to organize the club.[30] Hereford first organized a Board of Trade in 1903, which was reorganized in 1907 as the Hereford Commercial Club. Still active in 1910, this group underwent several changes in 1911 and 1916. The 1911 reformation was apparently spurred by competition from a similar group in Memphis, Texas. In the same issue of the *Hereford Brand* announcing the club's reconstitution and election of officers was a smaller notice stating: "Memphis people are getting busy in a commercial club way. They have leased one entire floor of a handsome business building and are transforming it into one of the most up-to-minute halls in the state. The furnishings are handsome and every article of modern furniture necessary for filing and reference convenience will be added. While Secretary Reed is busy preparing an extensive advertising campaign."[31]

The *Canyon News* also kept watch on promotional clubs and their activities in other area towns. The creation of a "locating company" in Stratford received special praise for seeking to locate and bring in actual settlers, particularly farmers. The *News* recognized the benefits of such a group for Randall County and the ease with which it could operate. All that was necessary was for representatives to go "before the people of the Middle States strictly on the merits of their case—a glorious country and one of golden opportunities—only awaiting the actual settlers and home builders to become one of the finest agricultural sections in all the United States."[32]

Although Canyon did not establish a "locating company," the town's Board of Trade was replaced by a Commercial Club in 1906. This club established three standing committees, one of which was for publicity. The duties of this committee were to "formulate and distribute such literature and advertisements as will best place Canyon City and Randall county before the homeseeker and capitalist, and to eternally keep at it and never give up."[33] Boosters in neighboring Amarillo not only established a Chamber of Commerce with a Publicity Bureau but also organized a separate Business Men's Association and the Panhandle Publicity Association. The latter, created in 1911, was to distribute information about the entire Panhandle, for, according to the Chamber's description, Amarillo's position of "Panhandle Metropolis" would only be enhanced by increased settlement anywhere in the Panhandle.[34]

The businessmen responsible for the formation of these commercial clubs and chambers of commerce recognized the importance of increased settlement of farmers in the development of the area. No town business could survive without the solid economic base that agriculture would provide for the area. Therefore, agricultural promotion played an important role in all commercial club activities. Closely aligned with agricultural promotion were the efforts by these groups to establish railroad connections for their towns. These lines provided much-needed transportation for agricultural products and made farm profits feasible.

The promotional activities developed by commercial clubs to attract farmers and railroads included placing advertisements in local and national papers, issuing postcards, pamphlets, and films, and sponsoring special days, fairs, and agricultural displays. A few groups hired outside talents to direct their efforts. Lubbock's choice for secretary was Don Biggers. A well-known journalist and promoter, he also worked for the Littlefield Land Company and wrote for the Santa Fe Railroad's promotional magazine. While in Lubbock, Biggers was responsible for the organization of the Panhandle, Plains, and South Plains Commercial Secretaries and Newspaper Men's Federation. He also provided a series of articles for the *Lubbock Avalanche* describing both the town and county.[35]

The Crosbyton Commercial Club also took advantage of the local newspaper and placed full-page advertisements illustrated with photographs of harvest scenes. One such advertisement boldly urged the reader to "Settle in the Garden Spot that is the South Plains of Texas—Crosbyton is the place."[36] Even more elaborate advertisements were published in the form of brochures to be sent in response to inquiries and to be distributed at land shows and fairs. The designers of these brochures were able to take advantage of the art of photography through the newly developed halftone technology that allowed photographs to be printed cheaply, enabling boosters to fill their pamphlets with photographic illustrations.

The Hereford Commercial Club especially relied on photographs and even entitled its brochure "Camera Chat from Hereford." Emphasizing that the Commercial Club had "nothing to sell—our business is to dispense information," the club's brochure alternated pages of text with pictures. In order to use as many photographs as possible, almost half of the pages were composed of six or seven small pictures linked together. Included in this brochure were photographs of orchards, various types of livestock, fields of crops, educational institutions, fine homes, the train depot, tree-shaded picnics, and carloads of immigrants. The accompanying text assured interested parties that the water supply came from an "everlasting stream of clear, pure, freestone water" and that 18.2 inches of rainfall "comes between April and September, when it is most needed for crops." Soils were identified as being of several types ranging from light chocolate to black sandy, and crops of all types were deemed suitable. In addition to the agricultural possibilities, educational and social advantages were highlighted, with a full page devoted to Hereford College. References were also made to homes with "beautiful Kentucky Blue Grass lawns," new sidewalks, one hundred automobiles, no saloons or "disreputable joints," "a magnificent school system," and seven religious denominations.[37]

The brochures for other area towns varied only slightly from this format. Some groups, like the Hurley Commercial Club, emphasized the agricultural aspects such as soil, water, crops, and climate, while others preferred a more eloquent approach, sparing few adjectives to describe their hometown. The brochure of the Young Men's Business Club of Canadian characterized the town as "basking in perennial sunshine, flanked by hills of beauty, and overlooking the serpentine valley of the Canadian for forty miles with the far-famed Antelope Hills visible beyond the Oklahoma line." This brochure did not neglect to point out special religious influences, the country club, and recent improvements.[38]

Crosbyton's brochure, *Crosby County's Year Old Baby*, was published in time to be distributed at the Texas State Fair, held in Dallas in 1909. The State Fair was a popular event for boosters as it offered an excellent opportunity to reach hundreds of farmers and out-of-state visitors. Special displays of local produce were built and taken to fairs to show both the quality and the diversity of crops raised in the area. In 1908 the Amarillo Chamber of Commerce organized and sent to the Texas State Fair a display of produce from the entire Panhandle. A similar exhibit was created in 1910 for a land show held in Chicago. Each county was given proper credit for its crops but spared the expense of shipping a complete exhibit to each fair or land show.[39]

To emphasize local products, commercial clubs and chambers of commerce began sponsoring county fairs and special town celebrations. The Crosbyton Commercial Club held founding-day programs featuring barbecues, speeches, trips to nearby Blanco Canyon, dances, and, of course, agricultural displays. Hereford promoted irrigated agriculture with a successful water carnival in 1911, and the Lubbock Chamber of Commerce quickly organized a Lubbock County Fair in 1913. The Amarillo Chamber of Commerce also began supporting local land shows instead of traveling exhibits, realizing that local fairs had the advantage of bringing people into the area and into closer contact with local real estate companies.[40]

Just as the newspapers and commercial clubs maintained a high degree of cooperation, so the commercial clubs were willing to support local land agents. R. A. Terrill, president of the Canyon City Commercial Club, issued a special notice acknowledging the contributions of real estate agents in the Canyon area and urging community support of their efforts. Terrill was concerned particularly about outside agents, calling them "warts of humanity" and a "menace to legitimate businessmen." He concluded by stating: "I think that every loyal citizen of this town ought to bring forth every energy that he may be able in driving out these highwaymen in order that we may develop the agricultural interests of our county most rapidly. I realize that this letter may seem a little harsh, but I also realize that it is not nearly so strong as the condition demands."[41]

This type of loyalty and cooperation was a necessary part of commercial club activities. The very basis of club membership was the shared interests of the businessmen in the development of the town or county. This interest led to some competition between groups, but the ultimate goal of settling the Panhandle also allowed for united effort. As the Amarillo Chamber of Commerce noted, any

Some of the Products Grown in the Rich Valley of the Canadian River

Elaborate exhibits of farm produce were prepared for state and local fairs to attract potential settlers. This one is from a Moody Land Company brochure. Photograph courtesy of Southwest Collection, Texas Tech University, Lubbock.

growth in the Panhandle would eventually benefit Amarillo as well as the outlying areas. This attitude was shared by other area towns. The *Crosbyton Review* found space to praise new towns such as Lorenzo and more established towns such as Lubbock. Another example of this cooperative spirit was Don Biggers' federation of newspapermen and commercial club secretaries. Although this group was short-lived, its members worked together to organize fair exhibits and encourage advertising support from railroads.[42] Railroad advertising had much in common with that of the newspapers and commercial clubs. While few railroads had immediate local interests, the need to develop new markets encouraged railroads to conduct extensive advertising campaigns.

The contributions of these editors and businessmen were an important aspect of the settlement of the Panhandle and South Plains by farmers. They provided the initial encouragement and publicity to attract newcomers and later sustained the efforts of real estate agents and landowners. By their cooperative efforts they proved true their claims of the special friendliness of the area and helped assure the future they so eagerly sought.

3.

The Railroads

RECOGNIZING THAT their future depended upon steady population growth and the agricultural development of the area, the early settlers of the Texas Panhandle and South Plains quickly developed an intense booster spirit. Railroad companies soon joined in the promotional effort and greatly augmented the local campaigns. These companies also had vested interests in developing the potential of the area and willingly used their resources to become important components in the effort to advertise and promote this area.

Land promotion was already familiar and accepted work for many of the railroads even before the settlement period of 1890 to 1917. As early as 1854 an official with the Chicago, Burlington and Quincy Railroad acknowledged that "we are beginning to find out that he who buildeth a railroad west of the Mississippi must also find a population and build up business."[1]

This need to build up new market areas and to generate revenues from land sales resulted in the railroads becoming the principal agent in the boomer's frontier of the 1860s and 1870s in Kansas and Nebraska.[2] Granted lands along the routes of their lines by the federal government, the railroads were to use land sales to finance their work. The fact that they were building into unoccupied and hitherto unwanted territory required innovative strategies. Faced with the novel situation of preceding settlement instead of following it, railroad officials rapidly generated new promotional and marketing techniques. In describing this facet of railroad activity, David Emmons has observed that "the railroads could not sit idly by and wait for the marching legions of American pioneers to reach them. They had to advertise, to stimulate interest, to misrepresent if necessary, but always to sell their lands."[3] The zeal of these advertising campaigns for lands in Kansas and Nebraska often led to excesses which, combined with disastrous weather conditions, resulted in bankruptcy for farmers and railroads alike. The experiences of these years made railroads more cautious in their efforts at land promotion for the Texas plains.

This caution was enhanced by the fact that the railroads building lines through the Panhandle and South Plains rarely owned land in the area. Unlike other states, Texas had retained control of its public lands after annexation, so there were no federal lands to be granted to railroads to finance their work. While Texas did initially follow the example of the federal government in providing land grants, different policies were implemented. The land given to railways was generally not located in the area through which the line actually passed, and a provision was made that the land must be disposed of within twelve years. Thus, much of the available public land in the Panhandle and South Plains was awarded in the 1870s to railroad companies building lines in South or Central Texas.[4]

In 1883 the land grant program was discontinued, leaving the railroads building into the Plains area responsible for finding other means to finance their construction. Consequently, they understood that their profits from land sales would come only indirectly through the development of a stable and productive population. Farmers, especially, meant railcar loads of products to be shipped to eastern markets, and railroad officials had every expectation that Panhandle farmers would provide ample produce and trade. For as L. F. Sheffy has noted, railroads were "tapping what they believed to be one of the future granaries of the United States" in crossing the Panhandle.[5]

The first railroad to cross the Panhandle of Texas was the Fort Worth and Denver City. Beginning in Fort Worth and building through the towns of Wichita Falls, Quanah, Childress, Clarendon, and Texline, the line reached the Texas–New Mexico border in 1888. Officials of the line had stepped up their construction program in 1885 to assure that the Fort Worth and Denver City rather than the Santa Fe would be the first to cross the Panhandle.[6] However, the Santa Fe Railroad soon completed its line into the area and was followed in the next decade by the Chicago, Rock Island and Pacific and the Texas and Pacific railways. Experienced land promoters, the officials of each of these railroads quickly established or enhanced existing immigration departments to handle this new territory.

Smaller, short-line railroads, such as the Quanah, Acme and Pacific and the Crosbyton South Plains railroads, also began promotional efforts as they established their lines. Although much more limited in the geographical area in which they advertised, these firms helped open more of the countryside for settlement and served as feeder lines for the larger companies.[7]

In addition to the short lines and the major companies with lines in the area, a few railroads crossing Texas with no direct interest in the Panhandle or South Plains occasionally included the area in their promotional materials. The Missouri Pacific was particularly generous: its brochure applauded the completion of the Fort Worth and Denver City line and noted that "this opens up for settlement the great Pan Handle country, which is as fine farming land as the bright sun shines upon." Treatment of the Staked Plains area was even more eloquent:

> It shall be the chosen land, perpetual sunshine shall kiss its trees and vines, and, being stored in luscious fruits and compressed into ruddy wine, will be sent to the four points of the compass to gladden the hearts of all mankind; and this shall be our sanitarium, a huge hospital where the afflicted of all lands will come and partake of Nature's own remedies. They will breathe the pure and bracing air, bask in the healing sunshine, drink the invigorating wine, and eat the life prolonging fruit. Sickness shall be vanquished. The people shall die of age greatly prolonged.[8]

Although the majority of the other railroad immigration departments refrained from such glorious praise, they did invest heavily in promotional activities. The Santa Fe Railroad alone had an advertising budget of $50,000 annually, and in 1911 the *Hereford Brand* reported that "the Santa Fe System has made a special appropriation for advertising the Panhandle and South Plains country quite in excess of the usual amount set apart for advertising purposes in this section and will be expended in advertising the resources of this section of Texas, principally in farm journals, including some papers in foreign languages, with perhaps a few magazines, the campaign to be started in early September and to continue for four months."[9]

The promotional campaigns of the railway companies included, in addition to those activities listed by the *Brand*, placing advertisements in daily and weekly newspapers; publishing brochures, agricultural bulletins, and magazines; hiring special immigration and agricultural agents; maintaining demonstration or exhibit trains and experimental farms; sponsoring fairs; and cooperating with local landowners and real estate agents. While there was considerable overlap in the work of the railroads, each company brought its own style and techniques to this promotion.

One of the universal activities of the rail companies was publishing, with products ranging from simple newspaper advertisements to elaborate monthly magazines. The newspaper advertisements were placed in local papers as well as in the major midwestern and eastern journals. Since the local papers were often sent out of state and contained booster articles, the railroads could achieve the dual effect of national advertising while supporting local businesses. One advertisement placed by the Fort Worth and Denver City line actually promoted the role of railroads and their impact on development. Noting that railways were necessary to a new area's welfare and that "Prosperity Demands Railroads," the advertisement aptly revealed the sense of anticipation surrounding railroads and the coming development of this area. The advertisement listed new lines coming into the region, using such descriptive phrases as "already crossing," "soon to join 'The Denver Road,' " "now building," "expected to join," "which may meet," and "headed for." [10] The Fort Worth and Denver City was, in truth, advertising possibilities rather than realities and would continue to do so whether the topic under discussion was future railroads or crops. They, along with the other companies, were promoting untested lands and could only base their claims on faith and experiments. To add credence to their promotional works, photographs were often added to advertisements, and the advertisements were expanded into booklets and pamphlets.

Several railroads used their brochures to promote the entire state, such as the Missouri Pacific Railway's *Statistics and Information Concerning the State of Texas* (1889) and the Missouri, Kansas and Texas Railway's *Texas: Empire State of the Southwest* (1911), while others focused on specific areas within the state. Included in this category are the Fort Worth and Denver City's *Facts about Texas with Special Information Concerning the Panhandle* (n.d.), the Atchison, Topeka and Santa Fe's *Panhandle and South Plains of Texas* (1911), and the Texas and Pacific's *West Texas: The Land of Opportunities* (1907). Another category of brochures, represented by the Rock Island's *Panhandle Country for Beef Cattle and Dairy Farming,* the Santa Fe's *Farmers Make Good in the Panhandle and South Plains of Texas* (1911), and the Crosbyton South Plains' *The Farmer and the Railroad* (1911) addressed specific crops or industries.

Despite the variation in coverage, these brochures tended to share similar formats and were directed principally at farmers and their families, since the primary focus of the rail campaigns was to develop and exploit the agricultural possibilities of the area. Pertinent information was presented through photographs, charts, and statistics in addition to the carefully worded text. These illustrative materials were also carefully planned, serving not only to verify the written text but also to make the brochures more appealing.

Expanding further on the advertisements and brochures, several lines issued their own magazines and serials. The Fort Worth and Denver used its quarterly publication, *Official Time-Table and Gazetteer*, to present articles describing the country along its Panhandle route.[11] Both the Rock Island and Santa Fe railroads published and distributed monthly magazines. The Rock Island, responsible for *Western Trail*, later renamed *South West Trail*, often distributed 100,000 copies a month. The Santa Fe publication, *The Earth*, reached a similar distribution. Featuring both promotional and educational articles, *The Earth* introduced readers to new towns and new agricultural methods. While each issue covered a variety of towns and counties along the Santa Fe line, a special Panhandle and South Plains edition was issued in May 1911. This edition featured articles describing the area, specific towns, and profitable crops as well as brief news items concerning the railroad and appropriate photographs. Local newspapermen, such as C. W. Warwick of Canyon and W. A. Parker of Plainview, and the commercial club secretaries for Floydada, Panhandle, Lubbock, and Lamesa contributed many of the articles. Advertising was limited to the last three pages of the magazine and included a two-column "Limited List of Southwestern Land Men."

Recognizing the public distrust of railroad promotion in even the most appealing brochure, many of these publications, whether brief pamphlets or lengthy tracts, contained statements on the trustworthiness of their work.[12] The Fort Worth and Denver City brochure *Facts about Texas* opened with this assurance:

> In giving the following information about the State of Texas, especially the country tributary to this railroad, we desire to make only a plain and honest statement of FACTS that will attract attention of emigrants and of capitalists, and that will be verified in every particular should they be led thereby to come to the State, either for a home or for investment.
>
> Texas has such vast and varied resources, and offers such a variety of advantages, that exaggeration is as needless as it would be unjust in this connection. By dealing frankly with the visitor and the homeseeker we seek to inspire a confidence that

will be strengthened by their own actual inspection and experience. We thus hope to induce an immigration of substantial citizens rather than of adventurers and speculators, who will aid in building up the country and developing the industries along the line of our railway. [13]

While an occasional lapse into the flowery language used in promotional materials for Kansas and Nebraska occurred in publications for the Panhandle and South Plains of Texas, the general tone was more conservative and open. The Fort Worth and Denver City also attempted to balance current problems with future possibilities:

The prairie fires which in years past have swept this region have prevented the growth of timber, except in the canyons and in the immediate vicinity of the numerous streams and springs, where cedar, cottonwood and hackberry grow rapidly . . . The problem of cheap fuel and lumber which otherwise would be a most serious one for the settler, will be solved by the building of the railroads now under construction toward and through the Pan Handle. . . . Meantime the products of the farmer will be in such demand from mining and lumber regions, at highly remunerative prices, as to amply repay the settler for two or three years of hardship and toil which are incident to any new country. [14]

Joining in this campaign, the Crosbyton South Plains Railroad subtitled its brochure "Cooperation for Profit" and emphasized the benefits of past cooperation between farmers and railroads. The railroads' role in land settlement was portrayed as one of enlightened self-interest, with corporate profits never outweighing the benefits brought to farmers. Acknowledging the railroad's part in the tradition of opening new lands and opportunities, the Crosbyton South Plains proclaimed, "The railroad must have the freight to survive and the farmer is the man to produce that freight. That's why we want him. The future of the railroads is the big consideration with us." [15] This candidness actually belied the full interest of this railroad; because of its connection with the CB Livestock Company, the Crosbyton South Plains was one of the few railroads to profit directly from land sales.

This brochure was also guilty of another overstatement. In the tradition of confusing expectations with actual conditions, the Crosbyton area was generously designated as the "Orchard Belt." Proof of the appropriateness of this title was limited to assurances that the area soon would be recognized as such and that all the requisite physical conditions existed. The officers of the Crosbyton South Plains were careful to support their hopeful claims of ideal conditions with statistics, charts, and testimonials, as did representatives of other lines.

Intent upon attracting farmers, the railroads concentrated on describing and highlighting the agricultural possibilities of the area. As with the literature produced by the local boosters, topics such as soil types, natural ground covers, climate, water, rainfall, and the growing of specific crops were presented. The checklist of recommended crops included wheat, oats, milo maize, sweet sorghum, kafir corn, cotton, and alfalfa. Alfalfa was especially popular with railroads and was considered to be "destined ultimately to rival the big staples as a revenue producer."[16]

Kafir corn and milo maize were recommended over traditional midwestern corn, as the yields per acre were significantly better and a European market for these crops was well established. Cotton received increasing attention as new breeds and machinery became available. Few statistics existed to prove its profitability, but expectations were high. Once again future farmers were assured that all the necessary physical conditions existed to allow for every success with the crop.

Any lack of statistics was compensated for through the use of success stories and testimonials from area farmers. J. W. Steele, commissioner of Southwestern Lines' colonization agency, attracted letters through a contest. His advertisement in the 1 April 1903 issue of the *Canyon City News* announced:

TO ADVERTISE THE GREAT SOUTHWEST

Farmers, farmer's wives and daughters, school teachers, doctors, clergymen, merchants in the smaller towns, any citizen who has something to say, are invited to write letters and longer articles about the locality in which they live in the Southwest. The territory includes Arkansas, Arizona, Indian Territory, Louisiana, Southern Missouri, Texas, New Mexico and Oklahoma. Premiums that make it an object are offered, a set for each state and territory. Full particulars on the conditions of the contest, and a list of the prizes and awards will be sent on application.

The Santa Fe published one booklet consisting of testimonials and then republished several of these letters in later brochures. The letters written in November and December 1911 came from farmers in Amarillo, Plainview, Conway, Clarendon, Lorenzo, Abernathy,

Pampa, and Post. The writers ranged from farmers with many years' experience to newcomers and even one young college student. They described their favorite crops, farming techniques, and livestock practices. Other letters also attested to the possibilities of success even in dry years and to the presence of adequate rainfall and water.[17]

The questions of rainfall and climate were among the most important and difficult addressed by the railroads' immigration departments. Robert Athearn, in noting the railroads' success in dealing with these issues, has referred to the companies as "the instrument that killed or at least temporarily anesthetized the desert theory."[18] This assault upon the "Great American Desert" image involved not only the documentation of adequate rainfall amounts but also proof of the available ground and underground water resources and the feasibility of irrigation. The idea that an increase in population could cause an increase in rainfall, whether through the use of plows or the existence of railroad tracks and telegraph wires, was much less prevalent in the rail literature for Texas. Although this had been a popular theme in Kansas and Nebraska, by the 1890s the railroad immigration departments had shifted away from increased rainfall arguments and had begun emphasizing dryland farming and irrigation.[19]

Those brochures with references to increased rainfall, such as the Fort Worth and Denver City's *Facts about Texas* and the Missouri Pacific's *Statistics and Information Concerning the State of Texas*, date from the late 1880s and were among the last to be issued using the promise of increased precipitation. The Fort Worth and Denver City's brochure was the most blatant: "Steadily and surely the farmer is pressing upon the stock grower; the rainbelt is extending, as it has in Kansas and Nebraska, and in a few more years villages and prosperous agricultural settlements will stretch in an unbroken line from the Louisiana line to the northwest border, 1,000 miles away."[20]

The Missouri Pacific's presentation, however, reflects the transition to more practical counsel for water needs. Tempering faith with pragmatism, this brochure noted:

There are ample proofs to show that as the soil is turned and brought under cultivation, in what used to be known as the Great American Desert, that the rainfall materially increases. There is no doubt of this, and localities that once never knew the blessings of a shower from heaven are now visited by sufficient rainfall to coax from the ground a bountiful harvest. This seems almost a miracle in nature. But unless this Utopian idea is fully realized, there is no doubt that the most successful farming in western Texas and eventually, all farming in that section will be carried on by means of irrigation, as is practiced so successfully in southern California. This seems like a drawback to this pursuit, but it is really the only sure and successful method of farming anywhere. The farmer who can control his water is the master of the situation.[21]

To enhance their position of honesty and reliability, the railroads filled their brochures with rainfall charts openly borrowed from the U.S. Weather Bureau. While the annual precipitation of the Panhandle and South Plains averaged from seventeen to twenty-four inches, considerably less than midwestern farmers were accustomed to, this difference was easily explained. Indeed, the Crosbyton South Plains brochure interpreted the difference to be one of the superior attributes of the area:

> From an agricultural standpoint the most important factor is not the gross amount of rainfall during the year, but how the rainfall is distributed. When compared with Illinois and Iowa and other more humid states, the rainfall in the Orchard Belt may seem slight, but when a reference is made to the records of the United States Weather Bureau, it will be found that over half of the total precipitation in this section comes when the crops are in most need of moisture. . . . The winter snows and early spring rains make soil perfect for plowing and planting, so that every inch of rainfall during the growing season serves its purpose better than double the amount does in a country where the precipitation is greatest in the spring and fall.[22]

The relative absence of surface water was also quickly rendered insignificant with the discovery of underground water. According to Steven Mehls, "The South Plains became the land of underground rain, far superior to any other area then available for purchase. These same boomers, who with their previous breath had denied the existence of a desert on the plains, quickly re-evaluated their position."[23]

Brochures and advertisements quoted geologists and presented the idea of an underground and inexhaustible river flowing from the Rocky Mountains to the Plains. This river concept remained popular well into the twentieth century, although by 1914 the U.S. Geological Survey had published new findings disproving the theory.[24] The primary value of the underground water came in its usefulness in irrigation. While few railroads recommended irrigation to the degree of the Missouri Pacific, most recognized the practical value of irrigation and at least recommended it as a safety valve. Many of their reservations about irrigation stemmed from a fear that too much emphasis on artificial watering systems would revive the desert image. In their cautious enthusiasm, irrigation was a technological innovation that, while not really necessary, could offer distinct benefits. The Crosbyton South Plains brochure advocated irrigation "only in the sense of getting the greatest returns per acre" and then only for "a small part of our farms in Crosby County."[25]

The topic of climate posed a similar problem for promoters. Just as irrigation and rainfall patterns could be viewed as superior aspects of the area or suspicious signs of poor land, so the climate could be interpreted as excellent for crops or very uncomfortable for people. In describing railroad literature concerning climate, Steven Mehls has observed, "Some effort was made to turn the heat of summer into a positive factor, arguing that the high temperature benefitted crops and kept insect life to a minimum. All these benefits were meant to rationalize away days of sweltering heat in the eyes of potential emigrants."[26]

Generally the treatment of climate was divided into two categories: as it concerned crops and as it concerned people. The Missouri, Kansas and Texas emphasized the contrast between Texas and the Midwest in terms of growing seasons and market availability, producing visions of bountiful crops and high early-market prices. The Missouri Pacific and Crosbyton South Plains chose, on the other hand, to stress the heathfulness of the climate with the absence of lung diseases and insect life. Assurances were also made that the tales of northers and blizzards were greatly exaggerated and that these events were on the whole less troublesome than winter conditions in the Midwest.[27]

Well aware that tales of wild conditions in Texas had traveled east along with those concerning the terrible northers and that this generation of farmers did not consider primitive conditions a necessary part of new home lands, the writers of railroad promotional literature sought to reassure their readers about the social conditions as well. Good farmlands were not sufficient by themselves to attract settlers; family life and society had to be considered as well.

The Missouri Pacific bluntly acknowledged the worst fears of easterners and then asserted that "every Texan is not a mounted arsenal, that there are other inhabitants of the State besides cowboys and greasers, and that other callings and pursuits are engaged in besides herding cattle, raising sheep and shooting at sight." The brochure further stated that "Texas is filling up with intelligent and enlightened people from every state and clime. They are your more progressive neighbors everywhere, and it is not fair to suppose that the climate of Texas is going to transform them into desperadoes, when, the truth of the matter is, they are transforming Texas into a populous and wealthy State. Society is well organized all over the State, and presents every characteristic of refinement and culture." [28]

In the descriptions of social conditions, public education received particular attention with references to the large state school fund, the quality of the teachers, and the opportunities for higher education at local colleges and universities. Also stressed was the availability and prevalence of religious organizations. The Crosbyton South Plains brochure even hinted at "liberal donations together with building sites" for any congregations wishing to establish churches in that community. [29]

The Fort Worth and Denver City brochure also chose to highlight the significance of the Texas homestead law and the favorableness of Texas laws toward women, noting especially the right of married women to control property. The brochure declared that "not only is the farmer and the workman sure that he will not be deprived of his means of support through execution, but that the family of an actual settler will not have their home sold from under them if the husband and father is taken away" and that "the importance of such provisions for the welfare of wives and children cannot be over-emphasized, and they have had large influence in inducing the tide of emigration which is pouring into the State." [30]

In addition to the arguments presented in print, the railroads took advantage of their ability to move people and products to assist in their advertising programs. The combinations of transportation and advertising ranged from bringing exhibits to farmers and farmers to exhibits, to sponsoring fairs and arranging land inspection tours.

Railroads had recognized the value of fairs and agricultural exhibits in land promotion as early as 1852 in Texas and continued to find them useful in the settling of the Panhandle and South Plains. Just as the Fort Worth and Denver City pioneered rail development in the area, so it also led in the use of fairs. Under the direction of Robert A. Cameron, the commissioner of immigration for the line, the Texas Spring Palace Exhibit was organized and opened in Fort Worth in 1889. The exhibit was designed to impress prospective settlers, especially farmers, with the varied agricultural and horticultural possibilities of the area. In addition to the displays of produce at the Spring Palace, a catalog was produced containing extensive advertising for West Texas towns. Prospective settlers were encouraged to attend this fair through special reduced rates made available across the United States.[31]

While few of the other rail companies sponsored fairs, most encouraged attendance with reduced rates. The larger state fairs attracted the most attention, but the railroads also supported county and town celebrations. The promoters of Crosbyton's third annual Founding Day Picnic proudly announced "Excursion rates on *all* trains."[32] In addition, special rail tours of developed farmlands were included in many of the local fairs and celebrations.

These tours were one of the benefits of supporting local fairs; prospective farmers could see the actual lands for sale rather than just carefully selected produce. Recognizing the importance of getting farmers to the land, rail companies attempted to work with local landowners and agents and established reduced excursion or homeseeker rates. These special fares allowed farmers from the East and Midwest to travel and examine new lands fairly inexpensively.

The rates included simple reduced fares, refund offers if land was purchased, and more elaborate group rates, with Tuesdays and Saturdays becoming the standard travel days. The Fort Worth and Denver City program announced in the *Canyon City News* consisted of "round-trip homeseekers rates to points along its line. These rates are upon a basis of one fare for the round-trip for parties of five or more persons travelling together on one ticket and carry the privilege of stop-overs at pleasure points North of and including Vernon, Texas, passengers being allowed a limit of 30 days in which to return."[33]

Actually the Fort Worth and Denver City operated at a disadvantage as it could offer homeseeker rates only to travelers outside of Texas. Regulations of the Texas State Railway Commission prevented the company from offering special fares from points within the state boundaries, thus limiting the line's ability to recruit settlers from East Texas.[34] Despite such limitations, the excursion or homeseeker rates remained an integral part of railroad promotion. The announcement of one line's decision to discontinue its program in 1914 drew sharp criticism from the editor of the *Plainview Evening Herald*, who demanded that "immediate and strenuous action should be taken by every organization looking to the development of the Southwest."[35]

Few statistics are available on the number of farmers who actually

By Special Arrangements with other Railroads
throughout the United States, we
have arranged for

REDUCED RATES

FROM ALL POINTS

EXCURSIONS

to the

Orchard Belt of Texas

the

1st and 3rd TUESDAYS

of each month throughout the year

Private Cars With
Meals and Berths

Personally Conducted by

Representatives of the

CROSBYTON-SOUTHPLAINS
RAILROAD COMPANY

For further information, address
Land and Colonization Department
Peoples Gas Building
CHICAGO

Excursion trains usually ran on the first and third Tuesdays of each month. Many land companies arranged for private cars to protect their prospects from competing agents. Photograph courtesy of Southwest Collection, Texas Tech University, Lubbock.

purchased land after taking advantage of reduced fares. More easily counted are those who arrived by way of immigrant cars. A companion service to homeseeker rates, immigrant cars permitted farmers to move their household goods cheaply. The railroads would provide shipping cars at reduced prices and usually allowed for a caretaker to ride with the goods. Occasionally the companies would let the entire family ride in the car, making the move even cheaper—if not more comfortable.[36]

A statement of the Fort Worth and Denver City Railroad concerning immigrant-car traffic on its line published in the 26 January 1907 issue of the *Dalhart Texan* reported that "from July 1 to Dec. 31, 1905, 418 cars were unloaded; from Jan. 1 to June 30, 1906, 395; making a total of 813 cars during the road's fiscal year." These numbers reflected an increase of 229 cars over the previous year. The Santa Fe Railroad claimed even greater numbers, stating that "during the first three months of 1907, it arranged for transportation to Amarillo of 1,340 immigrant cars of two families each."[37] Nine years later, the *Lamesa Leader* noted the arrival of two hundred immigrant cars over a twelve-month period and continued to expect more to arrive.[38]

The railroads made no profits on either the excursion rates or the immigrant cars but considered these costs, much as they did those of their publications, investments toward future profits.[39] Indeed, the future success of the railways hinged on the immediate success of real estate agents and land developers in bringing in and keeping farmers. This interest led to the formation of such organizations as the Northwest Texas Real Estate Association. Founded by William F. Sterling, an assistant general freight and passenger agent of the Fort Worth and Denver City Railroad, the association was designed to encourage cooperation among legitimate real estate agents.

These agents were offered additional assistance through the various railway immigration departments. The Southern Kansas Railway published a promotional booklet on the Panhandle and then offered to "send out this book to lists of prospective patrons sent us by real estate agents in the Panhandle," and the Fort Worth and Denver City arranged to share over two thousand names and addresses of prospective homeseekers with area land agents. The Santa Fe also placed advertisements in Panhandle newspapers requesting readers to send in lists of names of friends back East to receive promotional literature.[40]

The Santa Fe included in its collaborative efforts the direct support of C. L. Talmadge, a Chicago land speculator. In this instance the landowners in the Hereford and Bovina areas, as well as the

owners of the XIT Ranch, were contacted, and options were se-
cured for Talmadge. He was able to sell some sections at higher
than normal rates with little protest from other land agents.[41]

The cooperative spirit of the immigration and colonization
bureaus of the various railways did not stop with assisting local land
agents but was extended to the new farmers as well. Essential to
their programs of advertising, supporting fairs and exhibits, and
providing special excursion and immigrant rates was the idea of
educational assistance for the new settlers. Once the prospective
farmer had been convinced to move to the area and even provided
the means to do so, the problem became one of assuring successful
farming.

Educational programs proved beneficial not only in assisting new
settlers but also in improving the public's perception of railroads.
Official rail concern for education was formally acknowledged in an
article by Theodore Dreiser in the February 1900 issue of *Harper's
New Monthly Magazine*. Entitled "The Railroad and the People: A
New Educational Policy Now Operating in the West," the article
detailed the new efforts and intentions of railroads. In a tone of
cautious praise, Dreiser welcomed this shift and observed, "If the
public has had nothing save greed and rapacity to expect of its
railroads, the sight of the latter adopting a reasonable business
policy, whereby they seek to educate and make prosperous, is one
which, if not inspiring is at least optimistic."[42]

Included in this new business policy were such activities as hiring
special horticultural and marketing agents, producing educational
materials and lecture series, and assisting in the establishment of
local dairies and mills. The expense of these programs was justified
through improved produce, better marketing schedules, and an enhanced public image for the railways.

Railroad programs in the Texas Panhandle and South Plains received considerable local support, even occasionally earning editorial praise. The newspapers provided ample coverage of rail activities and frequently published articles by the agricultural agents
of the various lines. The most active and best known of these
agents was Professor H. M. Bainer of the Santa Fe. When he was
not authoring articles on plowing techniques or crop cultivation,
he was preparing lectures and exhibits or managing the line's experimental farm near Plainview. His job, as described by a Santa Fe
brochure, was to "help the recently arrived settler master local conditions and to aid the man already settled to get maximum crops
from his farm."[43] His reputation and popularity were such that a
lecture scheduled in conjunction with an appearance of the Santa

Fe's dairy poultry and livestock demonstration train in Hereford had to be moved to the district courtroom. During the lecture he encouraged the farmers to diversify their crops and recommended planting "a good deal of maize and kafir corn, some wheat, some oats, a little cotton" and "raising hogs, dairy cows and chickens." He also invited area farmers to cultivate ten acres of land under his supervision.[44]

Bainer's familiarity with crops and growing conditions came both from his direct experience with his company's demonstration plots and from the reports of farmers raising crops for the Santa Fe. The Santa Fe, along with several other lines, arranged to give away free seeds to encourage the development of new crops. E. D. Skinner of Tahoka planted a ten-acre cotton field under the direction of Bainer using five bushels of Mebane Triumph seed and was able to report a bountiful crop of three-fourths bale per acre. Other farmers benefited from the over fifteen thousand bushels of Turkey wheat seed the Santa Fe distributed from 1912 to 1917. The Fort Worth and Denver City was somewhat less successful with its attempt to encourage the planting of walnut trees but still recognized the potential of give-away seed projects.[45]

The railroads also recognized the potential of new farming techniques, especially the "scientific methods" of Dr. Hardy Campbell.[46] The Campbell method of dryland farming received considerable attention from the Santa Fe line, with numerous articles by and about Campbell published in *The Earth*. Other lines, such as the Missouri, Kansas and Texas, developed elaborate exhibits and demonstration trains to introduce farmers to new equipment and ideas. One such train described in the *Reeves County Record* consisted of "an auto car and a flat car for the accommodation of live stock, a passenger car for good roads exhibits, three lecture cars, a dining car and a pullman" and included "farm exhibits, improved agricultural implements, good roads literature and other features of interest to the farmer."[47]

The popularity of railroad programs and the genuine enthusiasm for the benefits they could offer to farmers were shared and reflected throughout the Panhandle and South Plains. The arrival of a rail line was greeted with enthusiasm and quickly became an important advertising point for the town or county. The announcement of a possible Santa Fe cutoff near Hereford brought forth this hopeful commentary, reprinted in the *Canyon City News*:

This means that we will have from four to six passenger trains daily, whereas now we have only two; that the cattlemen, instead of waiting for days for cars, will be enabled to drive to the road and ship the same day. It will bring this section of the Panhandle immediately before the eyes of the traveling public and enables the homeseeker to get in closer touch with the country's resources. Those traveling to and from California will have an opportunity to also take a view of the beautiful plains which are just now attracting such widespread attention. In fact, the proposed change will place us just where we belong on the map.[48]

Such praise was also extended to the advertising and promotional work of the rail companies, and, unlike the efforts in the previous land booms in Kansas and Nebraska, this work generally deserved the compliments. Learning from their earlier mistakes, the railroads brought refined and well-planned programs to the Texas plains. The indirect influence of the uncountable paragraphs of promotional text and traveling exhibits as well as the educational programs cannot be easily defined or gauged, but, measured in terms of the dollars spent and direct services rendered, the impact of the railways on the agricultural development of the area was indeed significant. While these companies were primarily motivated by the need to realize new profits, they were happily successful not only in achieving that goal but also in earning Dreiser's appraisal of having developed a reasonable and optimistic business policy.

4.

The Ranchers

GENERATIONS OF writers have romanticized and enlarged the conflicts between cattlemen and settlers. While some antagonism did
exist, so did a cooperative spirit. Dime novels and Saturday after-
noon matinees portrayed the ranchers as the powerful enemies of
the pioneering farmers. The effect of the fictional works has been
to overshadow the full role of ranch owners and investors, especially in the Panhandle–South Plains region of Texas.[1] Indeed, the
cattlemen of this area were an essential part of the colonization
movement, not only contributing their lands but also actively participating in advertising campaigns and development schemes.

Among the ranchers and ranches affected by the land boom between 1890 and 1917 were the Espuela Land and Cattle Company,
the Francklyn Land and Cattle Company, the Matador Ranch,
the XIT Ranch, the Bar N Bar Ranch, H. B. Sanborn and the
Bravo Ranch, C. C. Slaughter and his Long S, Lazy S, and Running Water ranches, and George Littlefield and his Yellow House
Ranch. These ranchers or investors reacted to the arrival of farmers
in terms of their own interests. Some anticipated the change
and planned for new agricultural developments; others accepted
changes gradually; still others sought to maintain control of their
lands and resisted diversification. Furthermore, these attitudes did
not remain static, for fluctuations in weather patterns and in the
national economy helped decrease resistance to new uses of the
land.

Opposition, especially to agricultural uses of the land, took many
forms but only rarely resulted in the violence so popular with
novelists. Often ranchers resorted to legal manipulations such as
county seat elections and land rushes. While certainly bending

the spirit of the law, the cattlemen generally worked within its constraints.

County seat elections were a subtle but successful means of delaying agricultural progress. The town chosen to serve as county seat could influence much of the surrounding area. In Collingsworth County ranchers supported the townsite of Wellington instead of the farming community of Pearl City.[2] The latter quickly faded, and the settlers moved on. In Crosby County cattlemen did not create a new town but rather elected one group of settlers over another. Preferring non-Quakers to the Quaker population of Estacado, stockmen supported the town of Emma. Estacado, like Pearl City, quickly faded, and Emma became "very much of a typical western cowboy town." Hank Smith, one of the original settlers in Crosby County, has recalled the election and Emma's progress: "There was scarcely any settlement around Emma, its being strictly a ranching country. Thousands of cattle being loose on the range, the public well at Emma was a common watering place for thousands of stock that did not belong within twenty miles of town. . . . Its main drawback was in being surrounded by large bodies of land owned by individuals and corporations that didn't want their stock range disturbed, and vigorously opposed the settlement of the country."[3] The ranchers' success in delaying settlement at Emma was reversed several years later when one ranching interest began an intense effort to promote land sales and a new county seat.

Somewhat more difficult to manage and influence was the Texas Legislature. Increased opposition to foreign investors and sympathy for farmers resulted in new land laws such as the Four Section Act of 1895 and its revision in 1897.[4] The laws were intended to open more lands for settlement and end continual leasing by ranchers. To prevent currently leased land from being offered for sale, ranchers began canceling their leases early and then reapplying for them before the land could be offered for sale. Such activity became known as lease-lapsing and was formally challenged in 1901 when prominent rancher C. C. Slaughter was sued along with the land commissioner by a Lamb County farmer, J. E. Ketner. The final ruling by the Texas Supreme Court abolished lease-lapsing and opened the way for land rushes.[5]

These rushes occurred between 1901 and 1904 as farmers and ranchers sought ownership of the land. Since ranchers, as individuals, were limited legally in the amount of land to which they could hold title, they often recruited family members and ranch hands to

C. C. Slaughter's cowboys at the Gail land rush. Photograph courtesy of Southwest Collection, Texas Tech University, Lubbock.

claim adjacent tracts. As the number of people vying for land grew, so did the number of clashes. Courthouse doors became the sites for shoving matches and fist fights. Efforts were made by courthouse officials to forestall violence in their halls, including the building of chutes and special windows for applicants to push their claims through. This still led to elaborate means of assuring an early position in line.[6]

To ensure being among the first few, contestants arrived days or weeks in advance to claim their place in line, and as the filing date grew nearer, assistants were recruited from surrounding counties. Each side was clearly labeled with red or blue armbands, with red signifying the farmers and blue the ranchers. As the groups maneuvered for positions, local sheriffs and deputies maintained watch and confiscated weapons. The *Borden Citizen* reported the sequence of events at a land rush at Gail in March 1904, with each group being ousted from the courthouse at least once and the final victory going to the "reds." At a rush in Big Spring, cowboys representing C. C. Slaughter prevailed with a unique strategy. Forced to wait outside to file through a window into the clerk's office, they built a high-walled chute next to the window and defended their position from there.[7]

Although these rushes resulted in numerous bruises and angry exchanges, there is only one recorded instance of the accompanying violence resulting in death. The victim, James Jarrott, was a lawyer from Stephenville. Taking advantage of the opening for sale of a strip of land in Hockley and Cochran counties, he began moving twenty-five families into the area in 1902. Area ranchers threatened the settlers but did not challenge or disrupt the land filing on August 12. Then ten days later a paid assassin shot and killed Jarrott at a windmill three miles from Ropesville.[8]

Mary Blankenship, one of the settlers, has described the reaction to Jarrott's death: "We became more concerned about our safety now, expecting to be wiped out at any time. Our gun and Bible became the family altar as they lay side by side upon the same table. . . . Instead of being scared off—if such was the purpose of the foul murder—we became more intent and closely allied in our fight for survival."[9] Local investigations into Jarrott's death proved fruitless. The murderer, a criminal named Jim Miller, finally confessed to the crime in 1933 but never identified who had hired him. The settlers, including Jarrott's widow, all remained, and eventually the ranchers' hostility turned to acceptance.

Many other ranchers had already become resigned to, if not totally accepting of, the farmers' presence. Legendary cattleman Charles Goodnight was among the first to acknowledge the inevitability of agricultural development. In 1885 he responded to a reporter's query about ranchers' attitudes toward settlers with this statement: "They [ranchers] don't think it much of a farming country, but they are willing for anybody to try it who wants to and do so. They say that stock farming does not conflict with them, and that if it is a farming country farmers will occupy it and the cow must go. It is natural and it is right and nobody is foolish enough to fight the inevitable."[10]

Two years later Colonel W. E. Hughes addressed the same issue in a speech before the Texas Cattlemen's Association Convention:

> The ranchman, as we view him, has been an important factor in the settlement, development and civilization of the State. His domain was the arid stretch of country extending from the Gulf Coast north and south across Western Texas. . . . He caused the deserts, plain and waste places, while awaiting the husbandman's hand, to contribute to the food supply of the world. The ranchman of the plains was not to be a permanence. He never so considered himself. His mission was to precede the agriculturalist and stock farmers, and until a changed order to things should make agriculture profitable, or

James and Mollie Jarrott, colonizers. Photograph courtesy of Southwest Collection, Texas Tech University, Lubbock.

possible, it was his to establish and maintain, with profit to the state, a valuable industry. He represented as it were an era—an epoch—a step in social progress.[11]

Hughes discounted the concept of rancher-farmer strife. He assured his audience that "This is but idle talk. Those who speak so are not adept in observational science. A little time and patience will show them in Texas the rough ranchman transferred and softened into the stock farmer and agriculturalist as naturally and quietly as the Winter softens into Spring."[12]

The editors of the *Texas Livestock Journal* also provide evidence of early acknowledgement and acceptance of agriculturalists. A promotional Panhandle Special Edition was published in October 1887. The issue was claimed to have been produced in excess of fifty thousand copies and was headlined "A Country Which Is Destined To Be The Granary of Texas." Illustrated with sketches, the articles described the progress of the Fort Worth and Denver Railway as well as the many agricultural opportunities in the area and discussed individual counties. In addition, numerous advertisements were placed by land agents seeking clients for the Panhandle. As a booster issue, this publication was the equal of any newspaper produced by Panhandle editors.

Ranchers were also capable of boosterism, and since they controlled much of the available property, they quickly became an integral part of the land colonization movement. Again, most willingly joined the effort, while others were persuaded by changes within the ranching industry to promote their land as a new source of profit. Interest and involvement varied from selling land to colonizers to actively planning their own sales programs.

C. C. Slaughter chose to maintain his lands, participating in the land rushes and avoiding sales until 1907. Finally he was persuaded to sell a portion of his Running Water Ranch by land promoter W. P. Soash. Slaughter followed Soash's progress with interest but was not involved in any aspect of the promotion. Soash continued to work with Slaughter, selling portions of the Long S in 1909.[13] Like Slaughter, the owners of the Curry Comb Ranch in Garza County sold land to C. W. Post for his colonizing scheme and left him to develop the land with no constraints.

While ranchers could limit their involvement to making land available for others to develop, many chose to participate actively in the sales of their properties by supervising agents, planning promotional campaigns, and even developing townsites. Along with the attitude and interest of ranchers, the actual physical conditions surrounding the individual ranch often determined the details of the transformation from cattle to corn. The availability of adequate transportation, especially railroads, and the basic accoutrements of civilization provided by towns were important, if expensive, factors in attracting new settlers. Ranch owners and investors, recognizing the value of these factors, soon became involved with railroad negotiations and townsite development.

Because railroads had already made significant contributions to the ranching industry, assistance in land sales became an added benefit. Those ranches without rail links to cattle markets were also without connections to midwestern farming communities. Thus cattlemen welcomed railroads, first for increased access to beef markets and easier shipping but later for enhancing the value and selling potential of their lands.[14]

Ranch manager George Tyng was among the few to express indifference toward pursuing railroad connections. Working for the Francklyn Land and Cattle Company, Tyng followed the development of the Southern Kansas Railway and wrote, "We want depots and when the time comes we will have them. . . . When our lands begin to produce the railroad company will provide facilities for handling products. It wants traffic as badly as we want depots."[15] Tyng maintained an unconcerned approach to railroad affairs; several years later he commented on the practice of naming streets and towns after railroad officials: "R. R. officials come and go—Nichols has gone. I hear that Starkweather is going. . . . Panhandle has a 'Groom' Street. A new siding on the Choctaw is named 'Groom.' Identification with RR interests works both ways. Any names easily remembered, spelled and pronounced are good enough."[16]

In contrast to Tyng's indifference, Charles Jones, manager of the Espuela Land and Cattle Company's Spur Farm Lands, repeatedly urged the ranch owners to pursue the development of a rail line. He candidly wrote to a friend:

> I have always felt it would be a mistake to put land on the market until the railroad was a certainty and it is going to make a difference in both price and movement if this feature is not definitely decided. Construction should be under way to an extent that would satisfy people that it was coming, as they have enjoyed the facilities of paper railroads in some of these communities for many years and are skeptical. Our people will know best, but if there is reliable, straight information to give out on the railroad certainly it will no doubt be used by them for all it is worth—and that is a big lot![17]

He continued this theme in a letter to the ranch owners S. M. Swenson and Sons, assuring them that:

The arguments which are put against our land is first the price terms, no railroad nor possible market for crops raised on this account, no gins, no schools, no churches and no settlement. Of course the railroad takes precedence in the minds of all these people, and we had a good bunch of people in here yesterday from Cottle County, who said if we could guarantee a railroad within a reasonable time they would at once try to sell their land and come down, because they knew that if Swenson guaranteed a railroad it would be built.

The Swensons acted upon Jones' advice and promoted the construction of the Stamford and Northwestern Railroad in 1909.[18]

The usual assistance given railroads came in the form of cash bonuses and rights-of-way through ranch property. C. C. Slaughter, once interested in raising the value of his lands, even considered accepting the presidency of one company. The Panhandle Short Line was to have passed through or by three Slaughter ranches. Slaughter offered right-of-way, forty acres for the depot, and $50,000. Unfortunately the railway company promoters were active only on paper, and the line never materialized.[19] Major George W. Littlefield was more successful in his negotiations with the Santa Fe. He offered a $100,000 bonus and a right-of-way to include a townsite. This line, known as the Texico Cutoff, crossed Littlefield's LFD pasturelands. However, further negotiations were necessary to resolve the location of the depot and to gain approval of the town's name, Littlefield. The compromise required three streets to angle awkwardly through the town and an additional bonus of land. Littlefield also approached the Quanah, Acme and Pacific Railroad, but disagreements led to a stalemate and no lines were built on Littlefield's property.[20]

The Matador Ranch investors not only provided bonuses to the Quanah, Acme and Pacific and the Motley County railroads but also actively worked with officials of the former railroad to develop the town of Roaring Springs. A townsite company formed in 1912 included Matador ranch manager John MacBain as secretary-treasurer and railway official Charles Sommer as a vice-president. Sommer provided monthly progress reports to MacBain that detailed the expenditures and activities related to the town's promotion.[21]

Publicity for Roaring Springs was concentrated in Central and South Texas in the form of newspaper advertisements and circular letters to attract farmers. Along with the letters detailing the terms and current local improvements, a sixteen-page brochure was published elaborating on the special features of the area. An exhibit prepared for the 1915 Dallas fair also proved successful in attracting a number of inquiries. The advertising expenses for Roaring Springs ranged from $4,214.16 in 1914 and $2,981.58 in 1915 to $3,374.37 in 1917.[22] Additional expenses were incurred through land agents' salaries and town improvements. These improvements included a school building and eight parks with approximately one hundred trees each. Special reduced water rates were instituted to encourage further planting of trees and gardens by townspeople. In addition, local businesses such as the hotel and newspaper were given extra support and assistance.[23]

The CB Live Stock Company on the Bar N Bar Ranch in Crosby County rivaled both the Matador and Littlefield ranches in involvement with railroads and townsites. The company was actively involved in the formation of the Crosbyton South Plains Railroad and the Crosbyton Townsite Company. These companies were directed by a ranch manager turned promoter, Julien Bassett.[24]

While the Francklyn Land and Cattle Company chose to make few concessions to railroad companies, considerable effort was expended toward planning townsites. The towns of Pampa and White Deer were considered crucial elements in the colonization plan for the White Deer Lands.[25] Resident managers George Tyng and T. D. Hobart maintained a steady correspondence with trustee Frederick Foster, offering cautious advice for the towns' development.

Tyng strongly recommended proceeding "one step at a time" rather than risk a boom. While he expressed doubts about the ability of residents to care adequately for new trees and gardens, he strongly recommended providing a water system and schools. His approach to the school issue was particularly pragmatic. He wrote Foster, "An established school adds fifty cents to $1.00 an acre to all of the lands within four or five miles of it, that being about the distance that children can go to day school, with gentle horses."[26] Tyng extended his pragmatic advice to the issues of prohibition and county seat elections. Responding to Foster's interest in banning alcohol in Pampa, Tyng observed:

My sentiment is wholly in favor of restriction, in deeds, of sale of liquors; so much so that, if I could recall a single instance of its successful application, that sentiment might warp my judgement advising you to try it here. . . . I have to advise against putting unusual—perhaps ineffective—restrictions into deeds—Liquor can come here freely by any daily train from Panhandle, Miami or elsewhere; you can not prevent it nor can the Railway Company. . . . Prohibition will come here and to every town around here by majority vote and by election of officers to enforce it; under Texas law; within very few years.[27]

He also advised against an active quest for the county seat title for Pampa, assessing its value as merely "greater than that of a good blacksmith-shop and somewhat less than that of a first class school."[28] Tyng agreed to investigate the legality of an offer to donate land for a courthouse should Pampa be favored with a majority vote. While such an offer was apparently legal, Tyng would agree only to advertise it as directed and remained reluctant to otherwise support the proposal.

T. D. Hobart, who replaced Tyng as manager in 1903, also felt that a county seat election could be postponed indefinitely. However, he did not share Tyng's disaffection for advertising. While Tyng had recommended limiting publicity to short advertisements in local newspapers and concentrating on crop experiments, Hobart immediately began preparing for his sales campaign. As L. F. Sheffy has noted, "Hobart was not interested solely in the sale of lands; he was more concerned with the building of a colony of contented and prosperous stock farmers."[29] Along with establishing a hotel and promoting an agricultural experiment station and a Presbyterian college, Hobart encouraged Foster to contribute land and cash for additional school buildings and to help organize a commercial club for Pampa.[30]

Arthur Duggan, sales manager of the Littlefield Lands colonization project, shared Hobart's concern for a sense of community. The Littlefield Lands project was based on Major George Littlefield's Yellow House Ranch lands located in Lamb, Cochran, Bailey, and Hockley counties. Central to Littlefield's planned development was the new town of Littlefield. Duggan concerned himself with all aspects of the community, including teaching Sunday school classes, serving as president of the school board and as a director of Littlefield State Bank, and working to establish free public transportation for area schoolchildren.[31] Duggan also encouraged Major Littlefield to contribute land and funds to local churches, especially for the Mennonites. Displaying some of George Tyng's pragmatism, Duggan wrote, "The building of this church will help to strengthen the Mennonite Brethren branch of the church here, and I believe will attract a number of people to that immediate vicinity. We still have quite a lot of land unsold out there and if this church is erected, I will advance the price to $100.00 per acre instead of $80.00."[32]

The official opening for Littlefield was held on the Fourth of July, 1913, and attracted 1,400 persons. Early publicity assured newcomers of schools, graded streets, cement sidewalks, and railroad facilities.[33] While the auction of town lots was less successful than expected, the existence of the town remained a significant factor for farm sales.

Charles Jones anticipated advertising a small city as part of the Spur Farm Lands, and until the town of Spur was founded he encouraged ranch donations to the Dickens Commercial Club and to several local church groups.[34] The XIT also became involved with several townsites located on the ranch. Ledgers and annual reports noted especially the progress of the towns of Farwell and Channing. Other ranchers also supported existing communities near their property. Frank Wheelock and Rollie Burns of the IOA Ranch in Lubbock County helped to found the city of Lubbock, and Wheelock later served as the town's first mayor. H. B. Sanborn has been credited as the father of Amarillo, a community that proved more successful than the town of Knoblauch, which was founded on his Bravo Ranch.[35]

Along with the efforts made for railroads and communities, ranchers planned and underwrote a myriad of advertising projects. These often involved working with local booster groups and the established railroad programs as well as planning experimental farms and irrigation wells, creating fair displays, publishing letters, brochures, and newspaper advertisements, and providing sales tours.

In addition, outside agents working on commissions or options planned their own campaigns and assisted with the tours and excursions. The degree to which outside agents were used varied not only between ranches but also from year to year on an individual ranch. Conflicts between advertising styles and commitments often led to policy changes, but the cattlemen rarely suffered from lack of assistance. Real estate agents and would-be colonizers inundated landowners with offers and contracts of an amazing variety and scope.[36]

Few of the outside agents were involved in the experimental farms or wells, although the established crops made their promotional work easier. The XIT was among the first ranches to experiment with growing crops, reporting in 1885 a "fair crop of corn and millet" and that "the sorghum especially grew remarkably well."[37] The XIT farming operations continued during the 1880s and 1890s, expanding to include acreage in sixteen different divisions or camps and such crops as prairie hay, alfalfa, sorghum, millet, Johnson grass, kafir corn, rye, wheat, and garden vegetables. The annual report for 1888 also included a reference to a small cotton crop. The cotton experiment went well and led to the prediction that "with proper handling and fair seasons cotton could be grown successfully here."[38] Another experiment testing the suitability of several types of trees was equally successful.

The promotional value to these farms and crops was acknowledged as early as 1892. That year's annual report claimed that "the continued success of wheat and other crops in the Panhandle, is bringing this section (where railroads are available) into active demand for farming purposes."[39] Further acknowledgment of the farms' role was made in 1905. George Findlay, the ranch business manager, wrote an article for *Western Trail* that was later reprinted in the *Dalhart Texan*. The article contained the standard descriptions of the soil and climate as well as a disclaimer by Findlay. He wrote of the success of the farms and noted, "It must be remembered too that nearly all of these farming experiments are conducted on cattle ranches in a rather desultory sort of way, the farm getting attention as a general thing, only when the ranch work did not demand it."[40] The implication was, of course, that if crops could succeed under this neglectful care, an attentive farmer could expect record yields. The XIT also served as an experimental area for Dr. Hardy Campbell's scientific dryland farming techniques. Campbell was involved with the Farm Land Development Company, which was based on a portion of the XIT lands.[41]

Charles Jones, of Spur Farm Lands, and Arthur Duggan, of Littlefield Lands, also began farm experiments. Jones sent letters to various seed companies as well as to the state agricultural commissioner requesting samples and farming advice. He included descriptions of the soil and growing seasons to clarify his needs. Jones was interested not only in proving the lands fertile but, as he wrote one company, in being "safe in recommendations to purchasers of land."[42] Perhaps the most significant contribution made by Jones and the Swensons was the establishment of an agricultural experiment station. The Swensons agreed to donate 160 acres of land and $3,000 to assure the location of a station near Spur.[43]

Duggan also devoted considerable effort to establishing a twelve-acre demonstration farm prior to the Fourth of July grand opening. Along with the rows of crops an experimental well was drilled for the farm. The well produced excellent drinking water but could not produce sufficient water for irrigation. This farm was not maintained, and in the spring of 1915 renewed efforts toward a demonstration farm began. The purpose of this farm was to showcase the variety of produce that could be grown in the area. Further proof of horticultural possibilities was provided by Duggan's wife, who surrounded their home with trees, shrubs, flowers, and vegetables. Duggan regularly brought prospective farmers to see his home as part of the sales tour.[44]

Using an imaginative approach, T. D. Hobart took advantage of the railroads and incoming farmers crossing White Deer lands and built a booth near the tracks to display his agricultural produce. The display did not find favor with competing land agents responsible for neighboring tracts. Unable to prevent their "prospects" from viewing the booth, a few agents resorted to vandalism and damaged the booth twice. Hobart persisted in his efforts and with the assistance of the sheriff and the Santa Fe officials continued to attract farmers through the display. He also took advantage of the farming experiments of the XIT and of early settlers by gathering testimonials about their successes. These testimonials were then published in the promotional booklet for White Deer Lands.[45]

While Hobart approached experimental farms in a slightly different manner, he shared Jones' and Duggan's attention to detail. Each of these men, and indeed the majority of ranch managers involved in land sales, felt a serious obligation to be fair and honest with settlers. Although their first responsibility was to ensure a profit for the ranch owners and investors, few managers sought this profit by deception or fraud. Most honestly believed in the possibilities of the land and of the communities they helped build.

Dissatisfaction with the quality of the land sales conducted by outside agents led the XIT managers to organize their own land company. Agents such as George Wright of Kansas City and James Pomeroy of the Farm Land Development Company actively worked the XIT lands, but sales were too often to speculators rather than settlers. Preferring to see the land developed by farmers, the XIT company instituted a new policy in 1905. F. W. Wilsey was hired as the company's land commissioner, and Judge J. D. Hamlin served as resident representative in Farwell. The XIT continued to use outside agents to bring prospects to the ranch but discontinued the practice of allowing options on large tracts of land. The land commissioner supervised the hotel built for housing the excursion groups, planned the publication of promotional materials, and worked with various railroad colonization departments.[46] The XIT also continued to send displays to agricultural fairs and in 1907 donated special prizes for the National Corn Exposition. Four free 160-acre tracts were offered, to be awarded by a committee of judges; the only condition was that the winners "must improve it and have it occupied inside of one year from the time it is awarded, and continue in its occupancy and improvement for a period of at least three years."[47]

H. B. Sanborn similarly experienced difficulties with outside agents during the sale of his Bravo Ranch property. He granted contracts to several agencies over a period of years and at one point had two businesses, the Browning Land Company and the Knoblauch Land Company, operating in the same territory. Both firms produced their own advertising material and were responsible for organizing excursion groups from the Midwest. In addition, each used the ranch headquarters as a base when escorting prospects but sold the land at different prices and terms. This arrangement not only confused the prospects but strained the facilities at ranch headquarters. One ranch staff member complained that the headquarters was left in disarray after each visit, that "our yard is usually littered up with cigar boxes, tobacco bags, etc. That our lanterns are nearly all smokey. That our rigs are loaded with cactus, rock, dirt and such things as strangers to this country are liable to collect and leave lying around." He further reported that the excursion groups were responsible for half of the current grocery bills and that five woolen blankets and one cotton blanket had disappeared during an excursion.[48] These difficulties were resolved after Sanborn canceled his contract with the Browning Land Company in September 1908. While he continued to rely on outside agents to sell the ranch, no similar conflicts occurred.

Arthur Duggan was even more successful in his supervision of the various agencies contracted to assist with land sales for Littlefield Lands. As sales manager Duggan was responsible for arranging advertisements, planning the town of Littlefield, supervising work on demonstration farms and wells, and organizing sales. Initially Duggan responded to each letter of inquiry and greeted the prospectors. His efforts were highly praised in the *Littlefield News* but quickly grew difficult to maintain. In the fall of 1912 Don Biggers, a well-known journalist, was hired to handle promotional work, and the first contracts were arranged with outside land companies. These companies generally worked on commissions and provided additional advertising and excursion programs. The Rawlings-Knapp Realty Company of Kansas City, Missouri, one of the most active firms for the Littlefield Lands, published an elaborate brochure and established a network of field agents in the Midwest. Relying heavily upon excursion trains, Rawlings added the innovation of music. Prospective farmers were entertained during the trip with songs about Littlefield that Rawlings had composed. The songs helped relieve the tedium of the long trips and raised enthusiasm for land sales. Techniques of other agents included arranging for full-page advertisements in midwestern papers and hosting banquets for the visiting farmers.[49]

At least two ranching operations refused all contracts with outside companies. T. D. Hobart at White Deer Lands and Charles Jones at Spur Farm Lands supervised all sales directly. Local agents were hired to escort prospects, but they operated under the guidance of Hobart or Jones.[50] The Spur Farm Lands also avoided the use of excursion trains. Arrangements were made, however, for hacks and tents for use by touring farmers. Jones ordered a new three-seated Hesse hack to be used along with the ranch's old two-seater and gave his wife detailed instructions for purchasing cots, cot bedding, inside tent equipment, kitchen and dining room utensils, and "china" for the ten fourteen-by-fourteen-foot "hotel" tents.[51]

Both Jones and Hobart directed their respective advertising programs and wrote much of the text for the brochures and newspaper announcements. Hobart placed many of his notices in midwestern papers while Jones concentrated on Texas. Jones ensured national coverage through advertisements in the *Breeder's Gazette* and also made special efforts to contact Swedish newspapers in Texas.[52] Brochures were sent to all inquirers and to names gathered from railroad officials. The other ranchers used similar promotional techniques, combining newspaper advertisements and articles with printed materials and inspection tours. The printed materials bore a striking resemblance to those published by booster groups and the railroads. Copying the apparently successful formula, the booklets addressed such issues as the soil, climate, suitable crops, livestock, schools and churches, and transportation. In addition, the accuracy and reliability of land titles were given special attention in the White Deer Lands booklet while Jones suggested an addition to a Spur publication praising the role of the cattlemen. He wrote: "Much has been written about the withholding of tremendous areas of agricultural land for the uses of the 'cattle baron' and their tenacity in hanging on to them for grazing purposes only. They may deserve some of the abuse they have received, but the fact remains that had this not been the case, the lands would long ago have been absorbed, and the homeseeker of this day would not have his present wonderful but fleeting opportunity."[53]

Promoters also made references to ranchers and cowboys and their role in land development through cover illustrations. The

Bassett Land and Livestock Company juxtaposed three images—an Indian hunting buffalo, a herd of cattle, and a view of Crosbyton—on the front of one brochure, while a Spur brochure used a shadow image of a cowboy looking over a farm scene.

Once these brochures and letters persuaded farmers to inspect the offerings, ranchers discovered the need for increased attention to sales tours. Competition for land sales and the increasing sophistication of touring farmers led to the construction of hotels and the replacement of hacks and wagons with automobiles. Hotels not only increased comfort but also served to prevent a ranch's prospects from meeting outside land agents. The Spur Inn, which was built in 1910, no doubt proved slightly more comfortable than any of the ten tents provided earlier. Arthur Duggan arranged for an eighteen-room hotel for the town of Littlefield before the town's official opening in 1912. Accommodations and entertainment for prospectors were costly but, as Duggan noted, necessary. In a letter to George Littlefield, Duggan explained: "It is true that we have never made the hotel pay any dividends on the investment. This is probably true ninety-nine out of every hundred hotels in small towns such as we have here. We built the hotel not as an investment but as a necessity and I think we have been very fortunate in having it pay its own way instead of being a heavy loss as has been the case with hotels built by the Swensons at Stamford and Spur, the C. B. Livestock Company at Crosbyton and the Syndicate people at Farwell."[54]

Despite such losses, the ranchers and their agents continued their efforts with demonstration wells, railroad connections, and town celebrations. Indeed, their interest in new settlers extended beyond immediate profit margins. While the amounts spent on advertising in the total efforts of ranchers remained small in comparison to those of the railroads, the ranchers contributed much in the way of assistance to towns, schools, churches, and individuals. A continuous effort was made to provide terms and prices in keeping with the value of the lands. Hobart actually priced White Deer Lands below the cost of neighboring tracts, while Littlefield and Duggan developed an Improvement Plan. This plan allowed settlers to defer the initial payment by spending at least $500 on improvements during the first year.[55] Terms varied over the years—from the XIT's offer of a 10 percent cash payment with the balance paid over nine years at 6 percent interest to the Spur Ranch offer of one-fifth down payment in cash and the balance paid over six years at 8 percent. Land prices, as predicted in every brochure, rose as the various areas became settled.[56]

The ranchers clearly preferred to sell to actual settlers rather than to speculators or investors. Once the property was sold, the ranchers continued to work with the farmers and often allowed for irregular or delayed payments. Hobart granted extensions in cases "where parties are occupying the land and making improvements" and was praised by Duggan for his success in land sales. Duggan also worked diligently to keep settlers; his success is reflected in the foreclosure of only one farm in the Littlefield Lands. The XIT Ranch was not as successful but shared the reputation of rarely foreclosing on working farmers.[57]

Unfortunately these reputations did not survive the onslaught of dime novels and popular westerns. The full contribution of ranchers to the settlement and agricultural development of the Texas Panhandle and South Plains has been obscured by the emphasis on the brief period of conflict. While the transition from large-scale ranching to stock farming and family farms was not as smooth as W. E. Hughes' poetic "winter into spring" notion would suggest, cattlemen must be credited with much of the smoothness and success of this transition.

5.

Land Agents and Colonizers

REAL ESTATE agents and colonizers did not create the land booms that occurred at the turn of the twentieth century in the Texas Panhandle and South Plains; they did, however, actively define and direct these developments. Working in conjunction with local boosters, railroad immigration bureaus, and landowners, these agents completed the network of promotion and shared in the successes and failures of the towns and farms that began to dot the plains. Their contributions included not only facilitating the actual sale of lands but also providing advertising and educational work, special development projects, and an added enthusiasm for the area.[1]

Real estate agents followed the opening of lands and the interest of farmers. Once an area could be reached through rail lines or was shown to be a potential agricultural paradise, land agents flocked to it. Lubbock waited almost twenty years for a rail connection; when the railroad arrived in 1910, the town listed fifteen land offices. Dalhart, benefiting from the XIT Ranch colonization, saw the opening of nine different real estate and investment companies by 1906. This activity was repeated across the Plains as each new community became a potential site for land businesses and offices.[2]

All of these land agents differed widely in their approaches to presenting and selling the land. Although the majority sought to make a profit by matching the demand for new farmland with available property, other motives influenced the land-selling activity. Four basic groups can be identified in the selling of the Texas Plains lands: midwestern-based offices operating on a piecemeal basis; local offices operating on a piecemeal basis or with limited development interests; local companies with strong development programs;

and major colonization or development projects. Those involved with colonization and townsite development generally expected personal as well as financial rewards and contributed considerable enthusiasm along with their more tangible investments.

With this influx of sales agents, area landowners had several options in designing contracts for the sale of their estates. They could sell their property directly to a real estate dealer, or arrange for resident agents in midwestern cities to work on commission, or use agents as missionaries to promote land and encourage buyers to come to inspect and purchase.[3]

Those making contracts, especially to work on a commission basis, did not limit themselves to one contract at a time or to any geographic boundaries. Letterheads of land companies and agents often carried a curious mix of locations and types of property. The Texas Land Company sold "farms and ranches in all parts of Texas and Mexico," while the Texas Nebraska Land Company spread its efforts over the two states, and western land agent E. E. Anthony advertised farms and homestead lands in southwestern Canada, Montana, the Dakotas, Washington, Oregon, California, Mexico, Kansas, Oklahoma, Texas, New Mexico, and Arizona. Another enterprising real estate dealer, R. J. Becker, headed up the R. J. Becker Realty Companies, which consisted of the German-American Investment Company, Bohemian Investment Company, American Development Society, and Inter-State Land Loan and Trust Company.[4]

The variations in advertising techniques and expertise matched those of company size and territory. Some agents brought years of experience in real estate practice while others were as new as the country they sought to represent. New ideas mingled with old as land agents and owners competed for future citizens. Quite often the agents vied with each other, not over prospective farmers but for commissions and landowners' interest. Ranchers and others announcing land to sell were inundated with schemes and proposals, most typically from midwestern-based companies seeking piecemeal commissions.

Among the requests to help sell the Bravo Ranch was one from a dentist, R. S. Bayne of Henry, Illinois. Far from wanting a career in land colonization, Bayne desired a commission for helping a neighbor locate new farmlands in Texas. His eagerness was matched by another interested, if inexperienced, inquirer, Cora Cherry, who wrote to Henry Sanborn after examining a Bravo Ranch booklet, explaining, "I think I can find buyers for your land both in the different states of Kansas, Nebraska and Missouri—I

(*Top*) Dillard-Powell Land Company, Lubbock. Photograph courtesy of Southwest Collection, Texas Tech University, Lubbock.

(*Bottom*) Canadian Valley Land Company, Canadian. Photograph courtesy of Southwest Collection, Texas Tech University, Lubbock.

(*Top*) South and West Land Company, Bovina. Photograph courtesy of Southwest Collection, Texas Tech University, Lubbock.

(*Bottom*) Spur Farm Lands office, Spur. Photograph courtesy of Southwest Collection, Texas Tech University, Lubbock.

am somewhat interested in the 'Real-Estate' work and wish to advertise your land." She further requested, "Let me hear from you as I would like a salary for my first month or two and I could go over quite a territory doing good work."[5]

In contrast to these somewhat naive offers, many well-organized companies sought new opportunities in the Panhandle and South Plains. One business, the Coldren Land Company of Kansas City, expanded its interests to include Bailey County properties. For several years, before offering any land for sale, the company conducted tests and prepared promotional materials. Beginning in 1907, the company made arrangements with the Santa Fe Railroad to bring prospective buyers to the area. As part of its promotional efforts, the company built a hotel in Hurley to house and thereby protect its "prospects."[6] The Cochran and McClure Company also worked with a railroad, the Rock Island, but in a slightly different manner. The railroad helped the company to identify holders of large tracts of land suitable for colonization. Basing their projects on tracts of five to ten thousand acres, they sold the land through excursion trips. Groups of midwestern farmers were offered special train fares and were accompanied by sales agents to tour available lands. Apparently, planning excursions was easier than locating suitable land, and, on at least one occasion, this company found itself with a full excursion party with no definite destination beyond the Texas border. On this occasion the company approached Sanborn about getting rights to portions of the Bravo Ranch. In return for a commission of $1.50 per acre, the agents accepted all responsibilities and expenses for organizing excursions and showing the land.[7]

M. V. Kelly, an agent of the C. C. Calloway Company and later of the Kelly Land System, proposed a similarly ambitious scheme to Sanborn offering extensive advertising for a twenty-five-acre section. Kelley, however, preferred to represent the land for a commission of $3.50 per acre. Yet another company offered to place advertisements in "close to 50 newspapers" throughout Kentucky for a three-week period if allowed to bring an excursion to the Bravo.[8]

A more elaborate division of territory and responsibilities was written into the contract between the South and West Land Company of Chicago and Witherspoon and Gough of Hereford. According to this contract, the South and West Land Company was to bear the expenses of the excursion parties and to use "all honorable means to make sales of Panhandle lands," while Whitherspoon and Gough were to obtain options on lands and pay any

(*Top*) South and West Land Company's private car. Photograph courtesy of Southwest Collection, Texas Tech University, Lubbock.

(*Bottom*) Automobile tour starting from the Littlefield Hotel. Photograph courtesy of Southwest Collection, Texas Tech University, Lubbock.

livery hire required in showing the lands. The contract further stipulated:

> The South and West Land Company agree to sell Panhandle land exclusively and not work with any other land agents in the Panhandle, except with the co-operation and consent of said Witherspoon and Gough. And the said Witherspoon and Gough agree not to put any more agents in Northern fields nor enter into contract with other Northern land agents or companies only as agreed upon by both parties to this contract. . . . It is understood that all prospects and purchasers from outside of Texas are to be considered as customers of the South and West Land Co. and treated as if brought in their excursions. All business originating in Texas is to be considered as belonging to Witherspoon and Gough and the South and West Land Co. is to have no claim for any part of the profits upon this Texas business.[9]

As part of its advertising responsibilities, the South and West Land Company published a booklet entitled *Last of the Great Prairie Farming Lands*. This booklet followed the tradition of being well illustrated and covering such topics as soil, precipitation, crops, shade and forest trees, cattle, and land values. While no specific prices were established for these lands, the brochure noted that current prices ranged from $7.50 to $20.00 per acre and could be expected to increase. Definite advice was given, however, on the best use of the land. Readers were assured that "the man combining stock raising with his farming is the most successful man in Texas." In addition to this counsel, the brochure presented a rather novel inducement for farmers to choose Texas land—the state's homestead law. The law was described as "the bulwark of the home owner and husbandman. It has enhanced the meaning of the word 'home' for him, his wife, and children. In Texas more than any other place in the world, the house of the toiler, or the aggressive farmer, is his castle, and though he live or die, succeed or fail, the faithful woman who has worked with him, and the tiny baby in her arms, will be defended and nourished by the strong laws which were made and are enforced in their behalf."[10]

While brochures had the advantage of allowing elaborate descriptions and explanations, many of the midwestern firms limited their presentations to newspaper columns. Papers such as the *Des Moines Register and Leader* conveniently arranged the classified real estate ads by states. By 1909 Texas was garnering a considerable portion of those listings. Using bold type and slogans, companies urged farmers to "Come to the Sunny South," or to "The New California," or to "Make 100 Per Cent This Next Year."[11] These advertisements varied from short classified listings to quarter-page blocks, and while the majority represented local agencies, a few came from Panhandle offices. As competition grew between lands within Texas and between lands in other states and Canada, the use of newspaper ads became more sophisticated.

One example of this sophistication is the development of specialty companies such as the L. K. Lee Advertising Agency. Through this company Lee arranged for a land agent's notices to be placed in two foreign-language papers, Minnesota's *Tidning* and *Der Wanderer*. The primary subscribers to these papers were German and Scandinavian farmers, and Lee assured his customers that the surest way to reach this group was through their own language. He was also quick to reassure land sellers that the children of these farmers could handle negotiations in English, thus avoiding any language barriers in attracting and selling lands.[12]

Another specialty firm was the American Land and Exchange Company, which prepared an elaborate listing of lands for sale in a number of states. The brochure was distributed to real estate dealers rather than prospective farmers. For an added fee, a landowner could obtain a separate advertisement in the forty-page booklet.[13]

These services were available for both the midwestern-based agencies and locally established ones and were likely to be used by even the small local companies. As the number of offices opened and, in turn, the competition for incoming farmers grew, new tactics were needed. Local businessmen proved as creative as their eastern and northern counterparts. They developed special offers, expanded newspaper notices, financed hotels, and even attempted the planning of whole communities.

One company using the special offer or service approach was the White and Thorton Real Estate Company. This office advertised a locator service, instructing prospective clients to "write us exactly how much cash you have and what you want." The company would then try to identify appropriate properties. Their advertisement further encouraged readers to consider Crosby County if they wanted a home "where Booze joints are not run, where the highest moral influences exist, a place where your boy or girl can be raised without bad influences."[14] Another Crosby County agent, Bill Lamar, chose to style himself as "The Hay Seed." His somewhat folksy and ungrammatical notice contrasted sharply with more traditional neighboring advertisements.[15]

The Canyon Real Estate Company elected to use an entire newspaper for its promotional work. The company donated a series of photographs to the local paper to be used in a special four-page "immigration edition." This edition served as an advertisement both for the city of Canyon and for the specific land company.[16] Many other companies relied on publications outside of boomer editions of newspapers or newspaper notices. Following the lead of the railroads, a variety of attractive pamphlets and brochures were produced. A few companies, such as H. H. Lewis and Company of Lockney and the Ansley Realty Company of Plainview, provided simple lists of available property and their terms. Taking advantage of their position as investment bankers as well as real estate agents, the Ansley Company added some flexibility in price structure by specializing in exchanges and trades. Showing a most accommodating spirit, the company offered land at $12.50 per acre or would "trade for gilt edge brick revenue property in Fort Worth, Houston, Dallas, San Antonio, Waco, Oklahoma City, Kansas City or Chicago, but would consider other places. Owner is a little prejudiced against hotels, but would consider a good one. Might take strickly black waxy, highly improved land, or Houston vacant or improved property."[17]

Appealing to a more sentimental instinct, the Short and Williams Real Estate Agency included a lovely photograph of two young girls with the caption "Products of the Panhandle" and this reminder: "If you invest in land it is here as long as you live and as long as your children live; it is a legacy as sound as the earth and as enduring as time."[18]

The droughts of 1907 to 1910 shook the settlers' confidence in this "sound legacy," and many real estate agents and promoters responded by actively encouraging the use of irrigation. D. L. McDonald of Hereford, noted as the "father of irrigation on the Staked Plains," published a brochure entitled *Where Crops Never Fail* and based his land sales on irrigated land. Another of the advertisements for the McDonald Irrigated Farms proclaimed the benefits of his system and assured farmers of "water when you need it, any time day or night, every day in the year. . . . The most wonderful crop yields have been taken from irrigated lands."[19]

Other companies and agents investing in pumping equipment and irrigated lands included J. Walter Day of Plainview, the Walter and Perkins Land Company of Hereford, W. E. Armstrong of Hale County, the Coldren Land Company, and the Fairview Land and

SHORT & WILLIAMS, TEXHOMA, OKLAHOMA

Products of the Pan Handle

Land promotion brochures were often designed to tug at heartstrings as well as purse strings. Photograph courtesy of the Barker Texas History Center, University of Texas at Austin.

Cattle Company in Hurley. Although these companies met with limited success in introducing irrigation, their willingness to use new technologies amply reflected the pioneering spirit of the area.[20]

This spirit was not limited to farmers, for along with the agricultural development came support for urban development. Townsite companies became an integral part of the land movement, vying to attract businesses and settlers to complement the new farming territories. Indeed, as David Gracy has observed, "A town served as a nucleus for a promoter's activity; it afforded him a good place for his office; with a hotel to house his prospects, it naturally lessened his chances of losing buyers to competing colonizers; it provided a trade center around which people could settle."[21]

While a few towns achieved success as county seats or trade centers, many more flourished for only a short time. Much depended on the enthusiasm, planning, and financial stability of the townsite company. In a few instances the "townsite" was never more than a hotel and land office. Cordena, established in Deaf Smith County in 1907 by the Western Farm Land Company, consisted solely of a hotel. This company was apparently less interested in attracting settlers with promises of schools and churches than in simply protecting its prospects from Dalhart agencies. The little town of Findlay in Deaf Smith County, also established in 1907, was somewhat more successful in acquiring other businesses but was abandoned within three years. Without a steady influx of immigrants and a solid economic base, these communities served only as temporary way stations.[22]

The more successful townsite companies realized that towns had to be more than elaborate land offices and stopovers for touring farmers. Recognizing that these farmers were seeking not just cheap lands but also new homes and opportunities, land agents sought to provide attractive centers for education, markets and supplies, and other services. This often entailed advertising the towns as extensively as the adjacent farmlands and working to attract appropriate businesses.

Central to a town's charm was the name selected for it. Several options were available for formulating names with the intent of influencing settlement. One popular technique was to recognize benefactors or possible benefactors. Thus Littlefield, Soash, and Findlay held the names and—it was hoped—the hearts of their founders and could anticipate special attention from those patrons. Other towns sought special favors by taking the names of railroad officials, for surely no official could resist locating a depot in his namesake. One town even tried to incorporate the names of two rail lines, the Fort Worth and Denver City and the Chicago, Rock Island and Pacific, as Denrock. Faced with Post Office disapproval, a compromise was reached with the name of Dalhart. This name combined the county names Dallam and Hartley, whose borders the town straddled.

Yet another approach was to select image over financial influence or support. Not surprisingly, the image most often evoked was that of water. To counter the popular impression of desert conditions, developers chose such names as Roaring Springs, Shafter Lake, Spring Lake, Running Water, Middlewater, Lakeview, and Oasis. In the case of Shallowater, the promoters' original choice of Ripley, in honor of the president of Atchison, Topeka and Santa Fe Railway, was denied because another town had already claimed that distinction. After some discussion the name Shallowater was chosen "not only because a well could be drilled easily in the area, often hitting 'shallow water' at fourteen to forty feet, but also because the name would hopefully attract settlers by advertising the underground water conditions."[23]

Unfortunately for a group of Deaf Smith County developers, the name Blue Lake was also already in use, so instead of promoting the blue pools prevalent in the area, they resorted to honoring a successful breed of cattle and selected Hereford for their town name. The planners of Shafter Lake were able to obtain official sanctioning of that name for their town and attracted a number of settlers interested in the lake. The town did indeed sit on the shore of a broad, if shallow, body of salt water. Many of the northern purchasers eagerly sent boats down to their new property; only to discover that the "lake" was unusable for boating, being dry in the spring and fall and too shallow the rest of the year.[24]

Names alone were not enough to attract settlers, no matter how eager they might be to accept the promise of water. More cautious citizens expected solid development and the amenities of their former hometowns. Thus, even the smaller local companies made serious efforts to assure the stability and forthrightness of their town project. The Stratton Land Company, backers of Porterville, prepared a lengthy flyer proclaiming the special merits of that community. Along with testimonials from actual visitors to the site and offers of free rail trips, this flyer assured readers that the townsite was not "on paper only":

> The townsite has been cleared and smoothed until it is as level as a table. All lots are plainly marked by white stakes, streets graded through the town and highways turnpiked more

than a mile into the country, a post office established, a general store, a lumber yard, a blacksmith and a shoe shop, dwellings, etc. erected in and around the town to the number of 35; a telephone line installed connecting with all towns east and west, a $6,000 steel bridge built across the Pecos River, the entire vicinity has been cleared of brush and other obstructions, making the neighborhood appear very beautiful. . . .[25]

The reference to a telephone line was underscored by the fact that the nearest towns were outside the county lines. Trying to turn this isolation into an advantage, Porterville's promoters stressed the lack of harmful competition from rival villages and the logical ease of their town would have in obtaining the county seat.[26]

A similar logic was used in presenting the townsite of Olton. After acknowledging that the nearest town was twenty-five miles away, the brochure for Olton stressed that "every citizen is anxious to make Olton a city." Along with guarantees of a delightful climate with an abundance of ozone, the brochure resorted to poetic insistence on a bright future:

The Indian, the Buffalo, the long horned Steer
Have now passed from this mundane sphere;
For where once they roamed, OLTON will thrive:
'Tis the inevitable law, the 'fittest' survive.[27]

This theme of the survival of the fittest and inevitability of the farming frontier was incorporated into the advertising for the community of Dalhart. The Wagner and Killen Land Agency placed the following notice for the town under the heading of "Facts":

History has proven that every new country in its development must necessarily pass through a certain period of depression and dull times, a kind of refining process, from which comes stability and permanency. A time in which weaklings are weeded out, false estimates are uncovered, and shady business methods exposed. DALHART and The Dalhart Country have been going through such a process for the past two or three years, and now THE TURNING POINT HAS BEEN REACHED, and we confidently expect our town and country to forge steadily to the front.[28]

Earlier advertisements for the town noted the special advantages of the town's location in two counties. Dalhart was already the county seat of Dallam County, and efforts were made to secure it as the county seat of Hartley County as well. Although the dual appointment was never realized, the two-county location made it possible to have prohibition in one half of the city and saloons in the other. Town boosters listed this fact, no doubt hoping to attract settlers on both sides of the prohibition question.[29]

Even with the most creative tactics and unusual legal arrangements, attracting townspeople was an expensive and uncertain pursuit. In planning the community of Brownfield, W. G. Hardin and A. F. Small arranged for lumber and other materials for a school. After investing heavily in the town, they were forced to seek outside employment to keep their concern active.[30]

As the number of land companies grew and new strategies and campaigns developed, a few enterprises took the lead. These firms often dominated the local market or eventually grew to incorporate wider territories. Motivated not only by the desire for profit but also by the need to create new opportunities, these companies left an important legacy on the Plains. Men such as C. W. Post, W. P. Soash, Julien Bassett, and C. O. Keiser and the managers of the Texas Land and Development Company combined vision and land sales in well-organized land colonization schemes. While their efforts occasionally met with only limited success, their work was an integral part of the land boom years.

The land company founded by C. O. Keiser, Keiser Brothers and Phillips Land and Cattle Company, was based in Canyon and operated by purchasing large sections of land. These properties were then developed for sale. Taking a slightly different approach to mass mailings of newspapers and brochures, Keiser sent his materials to school boards and teachers in the Midwest and advertised in Chautauqua leaflets. He also encouraged new settlers to write to their old neighbors to help dispel lingering images of hostile Indians and isolated homesteads. Keiser additionally recognized the importance of excursion trips and worked closely with the railroads—even renting private and sleeping cars for his excursion groups. In 1906, he invested in two Buick automobiles to replace the more traditional buggies for conducting prospective farmers to outlying lands. Not only were the cars more impressive in which to ride, they also greatly shortened the distance from some farmlands to town. Unfortunately, those farmers without cars soon discovered the difference traveling from their new homes to town in wagons.[31]

Shortly after Keiser started his operations in Canyon, Julien Bassett began his work in Crosbyton and Crosby County. Bassett first came to this area as a child and grew up on his father's sheep ranch.

The family later moved to Chicago, where he made several important contacts that formed the base of his investors and helped Bassett to purchase ninety thousand acres of ranchland in Crosby County. The CB Live Stock Company, formed in 1902, managed the Bar N Ranch, the site of Bassett's colonization work. His operations also quickly evolved into townsite and railroad ventures to complement the sale of his ranchlands. Realizing the importance of these "civilizing" factors, Bassett continued to rely on his Chicago investors to assist in the development of the county.[32]

Evidence of Bassett's diversity of operations and local popularity can be easily found in the area newspapers. The 3 November 1910 issue of the *Crosbyton Review* contained three front-page articles extolling his activities. The first article announced the formation of two new companies to promote Crosbyton—the Crosbyton Southplains Townsite Company, which was to "take over all the townsite properties along the line of the Crosbyton Southplains Railroad," and the Crosbyton Company, which was to "take over all business interests involved in Crosbyton outside of the townsite interests, such as the Supply Store, the Crosbyton Inn, the Wigwam, the Gin, Garage, Blacksmith Shop, etc." Bassett was listed as a vice-president of the first company and co-partner in the second. The article also noted that as general manager of the Crosbyton Southplains Railroad, Bassett would be traveling to Chicago for meetings. The second article further discussed current railroad plans, while the third dealt with the moving of a number of houses from Plainview to Crosbyton by the Bassett Land Company. In addition to these positions, Bassett also owned a three-hundred-acre dairy farm and six thousand head of cattle and was president of the First National Bank of Crosbyton and the Crosbyton Telephone Company.[33]

Bassett's land promotion techniques included establishing a demonstration farm, publishing a series of brochures and newspaper ads, using excursion trains, establishing three townsites, and securing the county seat title for one of those three towns. Initially, the experiences of his father and other early settlers in the Crosby County area served as proof of its agricultural worth as photographs of their crops appeared prominently in sales brochures. While this system was adequate, Bassett soon designed a more elaborate scheme. In 1911 he began arrangements for a ten-thousand-acre demonstration farm to be headed by Judge L. Gough of Hereford. This farm was not only to test new crops but to display new farming techniques and encourage "scientific cultivation" as well. Included in this project were special classes. As described in the local paper, classes were held weekly, with "students" being asked to discuss farming techniques and equipment to encourage them "to think and mix brains with their work." While principally for the employees of the CB Live Stock Farm, all area farmers were invited to attend.[34]

Bassett also encouraged scientific farming in the various brochures published for his land concerns and through his adoption of mechanized farm equipment. Taking advantage of the numerous offices handling Crosby County properties, Bassett's companies produced a variety of brochures with a variety of terms. The Crosbyton Southplains Railroad issued *The Farmer and the Railroad,* which offered land on a crop payment plan that allowed farmers to purchase land with a percentage of the crops raised on it. The Bassett Land and Live Stock Company, in turn, was responsible for the booklet *Three Ages of Crosby County, Texas: A Land of Health, Comfort and Prosperity.* Farmers purchasing land through this company were offered terms of one-fifth down and the balance paid over six years at 6 percent interest. Yet another brochure issued by the CB Live Stock Company, using many of the same illustrations and descriptive phrases as the other brochures, made no direct reference to prices or terms but encouraged interested parties to write the company.[35]

Other offers were made through newspaper advertisements and articles, especially for townsite lots. The *Crosbyton Review* benefited greatly from the many Bassett and CB Live Stock notices, as did a number of papers in the surrounding counties as well as foreign-language papers in the Midwest. These advertisements and brochures, like those of the majority of land promoters, encouraged inspection tours. But unlike many of those promoters, Bassett had a railroad at his command. Thus he could easily offer "personally conducted excursions at greatly reduced round trip rates" and could even refund fares for those purchasing land.[36] Entertainment costs for the touring farmers were also absorbed by the ranch as prospectors were often housed at the ranch headquarters.[37]

Perhaps the most generous, if somewhat self-serving, undertaking of the Bassett operations was the moving of business and homes from the town of Emma to the newly founded Crosbyton. The true intent behind this offer was to secure the courthouse and county seat for Crosbyton. Several buildings were literally carried across the Plains, and Emma, having once taken the county seat title from Estacado, now followed that town's unhappy fate and also faded away. Crosbyton grew rapidly and claimed a population of twelve hundred just six brief years after its founding. Bassett was somewhat less successful with the two other townsite ventures of Lorenzo and Idalou. Although these towns never experienced the rapid growth of Crosbyton, they were spared the fates of Emma and Estacado and still remain viable communities. When Bassett decided to leave the South Plains area for new opportunities and towns in the Pecos Valley and New Mexico, he was able to look back on a county vastly changed by his program of land promotions and development.[38]

In contrast to Bassett's diverse interests, the Texas Land and Development Company concentrated its efforts on improving one portion of the Texas Plains through irrigation. Formed in 1912, this company served as a development and sales agency for a land syndicate based in New York. Responding to the intricacies of Texas land laws, investors led by Dr. Frederick Pearson established separate syndicates and companies to control and manage a block of property near Plainview. Selected primarily because of the availability of underground water this land was part of a novel scheme.[39] Pearson's plan was "to divide the land into farms of suitable size, install wells and pumps, erect simple farm buildings, break for cultivation one quarter of the area of such farm, plant the same with alfalfa sorghum, and then sell the farms in a productive state."[40] An ambitious project, it required considerable capital to fund the improvements and represented a significant investment in the area. B. R. Brunson has referred to this investment as "substantially different" from other projects because "it put capital into the region instead of taking money out; and it is of rather unusual historical significance because of the great financial ability of many of its backers and the complexity of its fiscal structure."[41]

As a land promotion venture, the work of the Texas Land and Development Company was certainly among the most organized and best financed. Although the constant demand for operating funds became a serious problem, initially the company managed extensive advertising to complement the planned improvements. Under the terms of the contract drafted for M. D. Henderson, general manager, the company agreed to pay for "the printing, distributing, mailing and displaying of such advertising matters and for publishing such advertisements in the newspapers, magazines and periodicals," to pay the salaries of three traveling agents, to provide automobile services, and to arrange for substantial commissions for both agents and subagents. The advertising limit, including stationery and office supplies, was set at $30,000 per year. Salaries for the traveling agents were $100 per month with a $25-per-week expense allowance.[42]

Advertising for the company centered on articles placed in local papers, notices in out-of-state papers, and brochures. Henderson wasted no time in arranging for publications and by March of 1913 had spent $77.79 on advertising in various publications, $2,846.37 on printed materials, and an additional $123.15 on camera and photographic supplies.[43] The advertisements and articles in the local newspapers not only served to publicize the lands but also evoked goodwill. While perhaps not earning the unstinting praise that the *Crosbyton Review* gave Bassett and his land concerns, the Texas Land and Development Company was recognized as a valuable enterprise and was given extensive coverage in the local paper.[44]

The out-of-state notices generally coincided with the arrival of traveling agents and often were used to announce their presence in a community. These agents were also equipped with the company's brochures, and some of the more inventive carried stereopticon slides to accompany sales lectures. The brochures emphasized the benefits of irrigation and its ease of use, quoting experts who had personally examined the Plainview operation. Unlike many local boosters and the railroads, the Texas Land and Development Company management did not worry that their interest in irrigation might be perceived as proof of prevailing desert conditions. Both Pearson and Henderson recognized the growing acceptance of mechanized farming techniques. The farmers they sought were those who would see irrigation as a means to control conditions rather than as a sign of weakness.[45]

The traveling agents and out-of-state representatives had few difficulties in locating and convincing farmers to examine the project. Excursion parties were organzied and tours of the company's property quickly scheduled. The company was able to absorb the cost of most of the excursion trains, but on a few occasions a fee of $25 was charged. Several thousand dollars also went into the two demonstration farms and the creation of Lake Plainview. The farms, known as the Pioneer Farm and the Demonstration Farm, served both as enticing models and for crop experiments. However, agents usually avoided using the expression "experimental" around the touring farmers for fear of negative connotations.[46] These farms fulfilled their purposes well, as did the innovative Lake Plainview. Originally conceived by the company's president, Harry Miller, the lake was to demonstrate the underground water potential of the area. Located just north of the Santa Fe station in Plainview, the lake covered thirty acres when pumped full. Certainly a unique land-promotion undertaking, the lake eventually became too costly to maintain.

By 1914 the company was experiencing difficulties, not only in maintaining advertising but also in fulfilling construction obligations. Advertising work, especially through excursion parties, continued through 191C, when the company underwent reorganization. The sales program was discontinued in October 1916, due in part to the impact of the First World War and the greatly increased cost of materials and machinery.[47] While the ambitions of the original investors were not realized as a land promotion venture, the Texas Land and Development Company still contributed significantly to the development of the Plainview area, bringing in hundreds of prospective farmers, providing considerable advertising, and continuing experimental work with crops and farming techniques.

A similar sense of vision also influenced C. W. Post's colonization work in Garza and Lynn counties. Seeking to prove the value not only of this land but of farm life as well, Post inaugurated an ambitious land scheme. Already well known as a leading cereal manufacturer when he purchased over 200,000 acres of Texas ranchlands, Post brought the same enthusiasm and energy to land work. He founded a separate company, the Double U, to handle the construction and promotion of a townsite and series of improved farmsteads. A thorough planner, Post maintained an active interest in the progress of his new company, and although Post died before the project was completed, his influence remained strong.

His plan included establishing a town, complete with parks, schools, and businesses, improved farm lots with appropriate housing, barns, and windmills, and, for a short while, rainmaking.[48] Less generous with his advertising budget than were the investors in the Texas Land and Development Company, Post emphasized the need for interested farmers to make actual inspections of the land and the need to invest only in the "right" farmers. Central to this project was the quality of the new settlers, so much so that Post actually required references from purchasers. A standard letter was sent to friends and acquaintances of a farmer asking, "Has he the reputation of being honest? Is he thrifty and a good worker? Is he in your opinion a good farmer?" A separate form was used to ascertain how much experience the farmer had and any equipment owned.[49]

While somewhat unusual, these requirements did not seem to lessen interest in Post's lands. They were advertised through circular letters, newspaper notices, and brochures and were represented by traveling agents known as "missionaries." The managers of the Double U Company were rarely in agreement with the managers in Post's Battle Creek offices on their printed advertisements, especially the brochures. Forced to answer hundreds of inquiries with individually written responses, the Double U officers requested a brochure to send with the letters. They were promptly informed that:

> Mr. Post does not think you need a booklet or any literature. He wants the conditions down there to talk for themselves, and you ought to write letters to promising prospects which will draw them down here to see what we have. . . . If I were handling the matter, I would emphasize the fact that conditions there show themselves that they are more impressive than flashy literature, that you invite the fullest inspection and recommend that no one shall buy land unless he knows what he is buying, that the only way to accomplish this is to come and see it, and certainly anyone who has read the advertisement through and is interested in coming to Texas can be brought there to see what you have and without any furore or hullabaloo your very attractive show can be placed before them.[50]

Continued demands for brochures finally resulted in a small booklet, "A Chance to Own a Fine Farm," which partially replaced the series of newspaper articles the company had been including in its letters. A remarkable feature of this pamphlet was its lack of photographs. They were deemed an unnecessary frill, and the money saved could be used on "personal contact." However, agents were supplied with photograph albums containing the standard images of the town and working farms to show to excursion parties. One attempt was made to replace these albums with moving pictures, but the idea was abandoned as being too costly.[51]

Post was able to capitalize on his manufacturing fame and the novelty of his colonization scheme to save even more on his advertising expenses. He received national and statewide coverage with articles in publications such as *Pearson's Magazine*, *Harper's Weekly*, *The Earth*, the *St. Louis Republic*, the *New York Tribune Farmer*, the *Crosbyton Review*, the *Texas Spur*, and the *Lubbock Avalanche*. Arrangements were also made to place testimonials of Post farmers in various railroad materials, further extending the project's free publicity. Advertisements were purchased in a few selected newspapers, most notably the *Texas Farm and Ranch* and the *Semi-Weekly Dallas*

News.[52] Every item was subject to Post's scrutiny, even the notice placed in the *Post City Post.* After reviewing one issue, Post advised the Double U staff that the advertisement "is practically worthless." He encouraged them to continue to assist the paper by buying ads but wished "you would write better advertisements . . . No flowery talk or superlatives, just plain facts."[53]

Similarly direct advice was also given for various aspects of the townsite's development. Since so much of Post's advertising policy hinged on encouraging actual visits, there was an added emphasis on having the property in excellent condition at all times. A two-story hotel was built to house visitors, and hundreds of trees were planted along the streets and in the "parklets." In addition, the town boasted of a garbage and trash force hired to help keep the city clean. Every effort was made to attract businesses and to provide for the needs of both the townspeople and the area farmers. Just as Julien Bassett directed the growth of Crosbyton, so Post and the Double U Company worked to create a model city. The sale of town lots received attention equal to that given farm lots by Post's agents.[54]

The use of these agents serves as one of the best indicators of Post's approach to land promotion. Generally referred to as "missionaries," they were placed in the field to locate prospective purchasers and were under strict admonitions that "no misrepresentations as to the character of the country or as to the plan under which Mr. Post is operating with reference to the sale of land, are to be made."[55] They were also required to send in daily reports with the names of suitable contacts for the company's mailing list. During 1913 and 1914 efforts were made to contact professional real estate agents in several midwestern states to act as representatives, but the project met with little success. While many real estate firms were willing to list the Post lands, few could meet his rigorous standards.[56]

Those agents accepted by the company were, however, most successful in attracting purchasers. The project never achieved Post's goal of being a model community—businesses failed, neighbors quarreled, and the rainfall did not increase on demand, but over six hundred farms and ranches were sold, bringing many new families to the Plains. Balancing the practical with the philosophical, Post maintained high standards in promotion and helped gain widespread coverage of the agricultural possibilities of the area.

A similar balance can be found in the colonization and promotional work of W. P. Soash.[57] Originally based in Iowa, Soash learned the land trade with the John Lund Land Agency of Minneapolis. As a land salesman in Texas during the years of 1905 to 1912, he became head of what was later acknowledged to be "one of the largest land companies engaged in colonization and development work on both the North and South Plains of Texas."[58]

Soash's approach to land colonization was to purchase large blocks of land that he could then break up for resale as farm lots. His first purchase, a tract of the XIT Ranch, was located three miles north of the town of Dalhart. In 1908 he moved his operations from the XIT to C. C. Slaughter's Running Water Ranch, which included lands in Hockley, Lamb, and Castro counties. In 1909 he further expanded his operations to a second Slaughter ranch, the Lazy S, located in Howard, Borden, Martin, and Dawson counties. Unlike many agents who handled lands in widespread areas on a short-term basis or for commissions, Soash maintained complete advertising and development campaigns for each project. His leadership and talents in promotion received coverage in a leading professional advertising journal of the day, *Judicious Advertising and Advertising Experience.* The article applauded his style and innovations in a time when other land-sale campaigns were becoming more conservative.[59]

Soash not only combined many of the techniques used by his cohorts but also refined them. One of the most important aspects of Soash's work was his faith in the lands he sold. This faith was reflected in his investments in townsites and local improvements as well as in his advertisements and notices. One of the first changes Soash made in his promotional style was in the basic newspaper notice. Under the direction of F. W. Nowell, general manager of the W. P. Soash Land Company, newspaper ads were linked to the traveling agent's visits to specific areas. Prior to the arrival of the agents in a state, full-page notices would appear in fifteen to twenty of the leading newspapers. While C. W. Post later used this approach with his missionaries, there was a critical difference in the advertisements used. Nowell, as David Gracy has observed, "replaced the common, small newspaper notice, indistinguishable from dozens of other common, small newspaper notices with eye-catching layouts covering one or two entire pages."[60] This style was carried over into the brochures and posters used by Soash, with advertising expenses occasionally reaching as much as $4,095.19 per month.[61]

Another significant promotional expense came from Soash's use of excursion trains. Not content with the usual railroad company offers or the use of only one private car, he began plans for special train service through the Rock Island Railroad. Originally, the rail-

Ad from *Golden West* magazine. The W. P. Soash Land Company was recognized as one of the largest land companies in the United States. Photograph courtesy of Southwest Collection, Texas Tech University, Lubbock.

road agreed to handle the land company's special trains without cost to Soash whenever the train had on board a party of sixty-two or more. The company soon acquired three private cars and rented a number of Pullman cars and was allowed to run its excursions on its own schedule.[62] In encouraging prospects to ride on a Soash excursion, a special invitation was extended to the "ladies," stating that they would not be "subjected to the annoyances that are so common on trains conducted by some companies. Drinking and carousing are not permitted on a Soash Special and the ladies will experience nothing but pleasure while our guests."[63]

While Soash's first excursion groups patronized the lunch counters and hotels in Dalhart, new hotels and towns were built to accommodate later travelers. The first hotel was built at Ware, a Fort Worth and Denver City rail switch. While its location was more convenient than Dalhart for showing Soash's lands, no effort was made to create a new townsite to compete with the XIT town. For his next venture, however, Soash outlined a complete community in Olton, establishing a bank and church but no hotel. Guests brought into the Olton area were housed in tents or lodged with area stock farmers. A more ambitious plan was made for the townsite connected with the Lazy S Ranch lands. Located twenty-five miles north of the already established community of Big Spring, the little town of Soash was to be its founder's new home. Soash invested over $60,000 in the town, building a large hotel, an office and bank building, and garage and securing telephone and electric light services.

Unfortunately the fledgling town could not survive the drought of 1910 to 1912. With the countryside devastated by the dry conditions, Soash was forced to sell his properties to other investors and move his family back to Iowa. While the drought destroyed his plans, Soash never abandoned his faith in the Texas Plains. He was involved for a short time in land sales in Crosby County in 1913, and in 1924 he renewed business relations with the Slaughter family, selling more of their ranchlands.

Soash once described the colonizers he had worked with before coming to Texas as men of character who "fully believed in the territories they were trying to develop. In some instances, however, the development work that most of the colonizers undertook was many years ahead of the times for such development. However, later years have proved that their judgement was right, as fine cities and farms now dot the territories where their early development work perhaps failed."[64]

Soash's description is also appropriate for most of the land agents

Soash, Texas, Fourth of July 1909. Special fairs and celebrations helped attract potential new settlers. Photograph courtesy of Panhandle-Plains Historical Museum, Canyon.

and companies, large and small, that shared in the selling and settling of the Texas Panhandle and South Plains. From the local businessmen to major enterprises, the interest and enthusiasm of those
selling the land as well as the earlier efforts of boosters, railroads,
and landowners led to even more "fine cities and farms." Using
techniques developed in the Midwest or through newer strategies,
land agents and colonizers created advertising campaigns that were
at once adventuresome and practical. The diversity of these land
agents allowed a greater number of farmers to be introduced to the
area, and the interest shared by many of these agents in new farming techniques and crops helped many of their farmers to remain.

6.

The Settlers

THE ARRIVAL of railroad lines onto the Texas northern plains, combined with extensive advertising, effectively opened the area for settlement and resulted in a surge of interest and immigration. The work of the railways and promoters was significantly enhanced by the continuing demand of restless Americans for new lands, especially agricultural lands. In particular, these lands held special attractions for those in search of new and cheaper farms, for those in need of healthier climates, for ethnic and religious groups seeking new communities, and for individuals desiring new homes and opportunities.

Interest in frontier areas was no longer limited to fiercely independent adventurers; indeed, by the turn of the twentieth century the frontier was the key to advancement rather than to escape. The majority of the settlers and their children coming to the Texas Panhandle and South Plains sought new lands in a continuation of interest in land speculation and ownership that has long been a part of the American national character. Paul Wallace Gates in "The Role of the Land Speculator in Western Development" has noted that most European immigrants "brought with them to America a craving for land. Land for a home and a competence was first desired; then land to assure wealth and social position was wanted."[1]

This motivation was apparent in the settlement patterns of the Texas Plains counties, even if the settlers varied from the traditional hearty pioneer. One Panhandle resident, arriving in 1913, explained his migration and that of his neighbors in the Slovak colony at Pakan in this way: "The reason for our being here is that we are all the sons and daughters of the soil. Our parents were farmers in Europe and most all of them were owners of small farms and homes of their own."² These immigrants also brought with them the desire to establish farms and homes of their own and to secure the same for their children.

Unfortunately for many farmers in the midwestern states, land for new farms was scarce. Those farmers seeking to establish sons or sons-in-law on nearby farms soon found that not only was the amount of available land diminishing but also that which remained was increasingly expensive. Lands purchased in the 1870s and 1880s for $10 to $30 per acre were being sold in 1908 for $80 to $125 per acre. This increase in property values served both to make obtaining sufficient additional farmlands difficult and to make the selling of currently owned lands more attractive.³ Concurrently, the expansion of the railroads and development of new farming techniques helped redefine the agricultural potential of the Texas Plains area and opened new possibilities for enterprising farmers.

The area's land promoters were well aware of the changes occurring in farmlands elsewhere and rarely failed to use them in their sales pitch. Typical of the admonitions and arguments were those of the Moody Land Company and the Spur Farms Lands. The Moody Lands brochure noted:

> There are no sources of accumulating wealth in this country to-day that will compare with the ownership of land. . . . The land of bright promise and sure fulfillment is good agricultural land. Land in this great West that is selling today for $20.00 to $160.00 per acre was a friendly gift of our government only a few years ago. The development of our country has been so rapid that to-day all of the good government land has been taken, and there is no more open to settlement. Land in the Northwest and Central West has reached such prices that the man of ordinary means cannot secure large holdings, while in the Great Panhandle of Texas this land is yet cheap in price; so cheap that a few thousand dollars buys not a small farm but a whole section of land.⁴

The Spur booklet emphasized that "The rapidity with which available farming lands are being absorbed is astonishing to the observer who studies, and the lands of West Texas are going fast, and when gone, the difficulties of securing good farm lands will be greatly increased."⁵

The sense of urgency in these and similar statements used by land sellers belies the deliberate planning behind most of the promotional efforts. For while farmers were the principal audience for land advertisements, not every farmer qualified as a desirable customer. Hoping to avoid the mistakes made in previous land booms in other states, land agents for Texas Plains lands attempted to discourage inexperienced or financially insecure settlers. Furthermore, few efforts were made to attract direct immigration from Europe. As one land company official explained, the preference was for immigrants "who have been in America long enough to understand the country and its ways."⁶ Most of the promoters accepted that the best profit lay not in speculation but in years of steady payments and good crop management and, in turn, organized their campaigns from that perspective.

This approach also required accepting the demands of the chosen or preferred farmers, for few well-to-do farmers were truly interested in leaving comfortable homes for the rigors of unpioneered land. Their desire to move was generally coupled with the desire to advance, to provide their families with new opportunities. This interest in the comforts and accoutrements of civilization is readily apparent in the letters of farmers and in the advertising responses of the land agents. Equally prominent with the questions on soil and crop conditions were those on schools, churches, and social affairs. Typical inquiries to land companies were filled with questions such as W. R. Howard's "How many inhabitants have you? What is your school advantages and what churches have representation?" or A. Fairchild's "On what terms can you sell me a tract of not less than 80 acres with a 4 room farmhouse, barn and windmill, close to school and church?" or Lizzie Kingsbury's "How near town could a farm be bought and is there a high school in the town?" And most important of all to a mother, "Is the town free from saloons and is there any provision made in the charter or town organization to keep the town free from this curse?"⁷

Land agents, in turn, openly acknowledged these demands and requirements of this new breed of settler. In a report to the investors, the manager of the Roaring Springs Townsite Company explained that "there are lots of people coming to this country to look at it, but most of them that come from the East are failing to locate, claiming that our country is too much underdeveloped. Most of them want to locate where there are schools and churches."⁸ Charles Jones, manager of the Spur Farm Lands, completed a similar report, noting that "we continue to have prospectors every day who seem to be in earnest, but finally decide to look further as cost of improvements and inconvenience so far from a railroad operate to prevent their closing at our prices, although invariably satisfied with our lands."[9]

Concern for the expectations of immigrants was also translated into advertising copy. Recognizing the civilized advantages of the Lubbock area over its neighboring territory, the Dillard-Powell Realty Company posed a strategic question: "Do you want to settle in a country where the hardships of pioneering as endured by the settlers of a generation and more ago, have been rolled away on the chariot wheels of the modern railway train, where all the advantages with none of the privations of pioneer life are to be obtained?"[10]

Bulletins and brochures regularly described the amount spent on school buildings, the number and denominations of churches, and the general high moral standards of the population. Care was also taken to provide photographs of healthy children, tree-and-flower-encircled homes, and, if possible, prosperous-looking business and church buildings.

A few land agents and owners even made special appeals to women. These appeals were issued both in recognition of wifely influence in moving decisions and as attempts to enhance the social value of a colony or land company. As early as 1884 references were being made about the advantages the West held for women, especially single women. Referring to a visit by a young woman to the Big Spring area, one brochure predicted that she would "probably marry a million dollar ranch man before she returns—for that is usually the destiny of attractive young ladies in this country."[11]

More often, special appeals were directed to wives with the intent of recruiting whole families. Once again the emphasis of the advertisers was on the modern pioneer, not the lone plainsman conquering a new environment. Indeed, C. O. Keiser of Canyon specifically sought to dispel the old images and rumors of terrible conditions on the Texas Plains. He actively encouraged new settlers to write back to their home states and describe social and religious conditions along with the farming prospects. Apparently much of the correspondence between new settlers and old neighbors was written by the women, giving Keiser an immediate advantage.[12]

W. P. Soash, in promoting his Big Spring property, not only invited wives to accompany their husbands on land tours but also urged "the husband and father" to bring their wives along. His brochure claimed, "We want the ladies to realize the land we have for sale is located in God's country, where every influence for all that is good is as pronounced as 'at home.'"[13]

Another direct appeal was made by the Western Farm Land Company of Stratford. Their newspaper notice declared in bold

Photographs became an important part of promotional literature, giving visual documentation to the written descriptions. Brochure covers courtesy of the Southwest Collection, Texas Tech University, Lubbock.

letters "Urge Your Husband to Move to the Panhandle" and continued, "Tell him that you desire an easier life and future which will be free from hardship."[14] This ad also mentioned private rail cars for tours. Private cars, originally used to protect prospects from competing land agents, also proved capable of protecting prospects from many of the rigors of travel. Land companies discovered that with private cars they could effectively control the atmosphere of the cars and thereby greatly enhance their chances of selling land.[15]

Advertisers found a responsive audience in women. While the majority of the correspondence received by land companies was from men, a number of women also sent letters of inquiry. They wrote for friends, for relatives, and for themselves. Mrs. C. M. Roberts was requested by "several respectable families" to seek information about the Post Farm Lands, and Mrs. M. A. Riggs of Duarte, California, wrote on her own initiative in behalf of "two young men, who were good workers, was raised on the farm and I would like to see them get a start again."[16]

The image of the farmland of the West as a site for new beginnings was a recurring theme in the letters of women. Widows and mothers sought a chance to hold families together or to provide for their family's future. These inquiries ranged from the highly idealistic to the very practical and forthright. While the innocence of some of the authors must have amused land sales offices, few traces of condescension were apparent in their responses. In fact, one particularly charming, if naive, letter received a two-page letter of response from the Double U officials. In this inquiry Miss Bertha Ingalls of South Hero, Vermont, wrote:

> What can you do with a young man who has several thousand dollars and no initiative? He is dying by inches in a New York office which the sun never enters. He has been there ever since he was 14 years of age, has no bad habits and is very industrious. The article about Post City in the October 'Pearsons' has moved me to write you, in the hope that you could show the way to an out-of-doors occupation, for this brother of mine who would gladly try farming except that he has no experience and fears to risk the certainty he has, for possible failure in agriculture. This article by Mr. Lack Moore has made me feel that you are the person to furnish the mental stimulus for the plunge.[17]

Clearly Miss Ingalls was less in need of a "mental stimulus" than was her brother, as she added a brief postscript stating, "If my brother goes to Texas, I intend to go with him."

Miss Ingalls' lack of experience did not hinder her desire for a move, and as conditions improved in the West so did the number of opportunities for women. The development of townsites and expanded modes of transportation made pioneering easier for women without the protection of family. Positions as store clerks or hotel managers created viable options for self-supporting and independent ladies. Those land companies advertising for hotel or boarding-house managers were inundated with applications, primarily from women, and those connected with townsites often received inquiries about possible occupations and wages for women "who have to and are desirous to earn their own living."[18] While the number of these women remained relatively small in comparison with the number of farm families moving onto the Plains, the very availability of jobs reflected the changes in American settlement patterns.

The journey west also appealed to another relatively small group of immigrants—those seeking healthier environments. Unlike the few enterprising and adventuresome women, the health-seekers were following a long-established pattern in coming to Texas. As early as 1828, claims of especially healthy conditions were being made by Texans, a practice that continued as an integral part of Texas promotion.[19] The *Texas Almanac*, which aimed to be "not only of real value, but almost indispensable to all recent and intending immigrants," served as a major source of health-related advertising from its inception in 1858.[20]

While the Panhandle and South Plains did not develop the major resort or sanitarium facilities found in other parts of the state, at least one community benefited from Texas' healthy climate. C. W. Post, founder of Post, Texas, first came to Texas in 1886 seeking a respite from health problems. From that visit an interest in promoting Texas real estate developed and eventually resulted in a full-scale colonization project.[21] While this effort was economically motivated, health topics were included amid its advertising of agricultural promise. The glowing descriptions of health-inducing sunshine and moderate temperatures offered by Post's company and by his competitors helped attract settlers seeking relief from catarrh or asthma or the rigors of northern winters.[22]

Certainly the advertisers spared no efforts in identifying and praising the climatic virtues of their various properties. The Dillard-Powell Land Company unabashedly proclaimed the benefits of the Lubbock area in terms of dire expectations elsewhere:

> The purity of the air together with its unusual dryness in the winter season makes the high Plains country a veritable harbor of safety to man or woman with weak lungs and a tendency to consumption. For many poor unfortunates living in a low altitude and damp and poisoned atmosphere, the sentence of death has already been pronounced if they remain where they are. And to all such the invitation is especially extended to come up higher. There is a chance for you to enjoy a long and useful life here. Remain where you are and your days are surely numbered. Do not wait until actually smitten with the dreaded tuberculosis, for then it is all got to be too late.[23]

In contrast to this stark invitation, the Rawlings-Knapp Company chose to highlight the neighboring Littlefield area in more positive terms, declaring that "this 3,600 foot altitude with its attendant glorious ozone, bright sunshine, pure exhilarating and health-giving air becomes near being the *fountain of youth* which men have long sought." Their brochure further stated that this climate could "cure a bad temper or a lean pocket book" and that "hypochondriacs forget their troubles and get a new grip on life, gaining a new viewpoint which makes for happiness."[24] These various descriptions, whether cheerful or serious, served to counterpoint the bleak images once associated with the Plains. In only a few years the area had been transformed from a harsh, isolated frontier to a haven for families and health-seekers.

Along with the agricultural and health-related potentials forecast by boosters, the plains area also offered spiritual independence. The first two attempts at organized settlements were actually based on religious interests, and while their success was limited, the door remained open for ethnic and religious communities.[25] Indeed, a number of land companies and agents made special efforts to attract such groups.

The primary benefactors of this interest were German Mennonites, Lutheran groups, especially Swedish and German Lutherans, and Catholics. While many townsites and communities were developed by local land companies, several of the ethnic colonies came about due to the efforts of individuals within the community rather than through professional agents. Among the companies expressing interest in colonizing folk groups were the Texas Land Company, Keiser Brothers and Phillips, Long and Lair, the Golden

Belt Land Company, Mance and Peacock, the Texas Land and Development Company, the White Deer Land Company, W. P. Soash, Rawlings-Knapp Realty, and the Anders L. Mordt Land Company.[26] The enthusiasm of these agencies stemmed primarily from pragmatic rather than philosophical reasons. Tom Rowan, part owner of the Texas Land Company, explained that most of these settlers were not only thrifty and industrious but also "not afraid of hardships, were clannish, and therefore preferred closed communities, with more prospective land sales for the land companies in the offering."[27]

In addition, many land agencies recognized that the very presence of certain colonies enhanced the value of their lands. Not only would these communities attract others of similar faith or background, but they were often viewed as good neighbors by other midwestern farmers. Recognizing this, the Rawlings-Knapp Company not only sought out colonies to bring to the Littlefield area but also used the actual presence of German Mennonites in their advertisements for the more traditional settlers. Under the heading "The Best Farm Lands," the company explained that "we have already sold enough of this land to German Mennonite settlers to warrant the belief that we will soon have at Littlefield, the largest German Mennonite Colony in the United States. They investigated our proposition most thoroughly and found it just what they wanted for colonization purposes and having bought are now moving on their land and improving same. There are no better judges of land than German Farmers."[28] In addition, the brochure contained no less than ten photographs of German farmers inspecting or working on Littlefield lands.

Few other companies went to such lengths to acknowledge the presence of particular groups or their implied approval, but many did conduct special promotions and advertising campaigns. The advertisements were basically adaptations of the techniques used for the more traditional settler. Agents placed newspaper notices, sent circular letters, conducted excursions, and made arrangements for constructing churches and schools. The newspaper advertisements appeared in journals such as the *Landsmann*, the *St. Louis Blatt*, the *New Braunfelser Zeitung*, *Nowiny Teksaskie*, the *Lincoln* (Nebraska) *Presse*, the *Decorah* (Iowa) *Posten*, the *Lutheraneren*, *Skandaven*, and the *Southern Messenger*. Three of these papers, the *Nowiny Teksaskie*, the *New Braunfelser Zeitung*, and the *Southern Messenger*, were published in Central or South Texas. Another paper, the *Oslo Posten*, was designed specifically to boost the colony and townsite of Oslo in Hansford County and was distributed throughout the

Midwest.[29]

Along with foreign-language notices, agents also sent thousands of circular letters to German Catholic and Amish groups. These letters proved successful in several instances, especially for Father Joseph Reisdorff, a Catholic priest with a strong interest in land promotion. In recruiting German Catholics for the Western Investment Company's townsite of Slaton, Reisdorff and his partner, M. F. Klattenhoff, were able to recruit both German Catholics from the Midwest and German Lutherans from Central Texas, selling over $40,000 worth of land in less than a year.[30]

Adding a more personal touch were tours through the Midwest by land salesmen and escorted inspection tours. Victor Wallin of the Wallin and Johnson Land Company visited farming communities and gave lectures accompanied by stereopticon slides; on occasion he even recruited local priests to function as subagents, lending a form of official sanctioning to his ventures.[31] Farmers or selected representatives were also invited to inspect land holdings. Frequently only one or two farmers would tour the properties and then report back to their home communities. The settlements at Rhea, White Deer, and Nazareth all stemmed from visits by individuals who later assisted land agents in encouraging their neighbors to move to the Plains.[32]

Just as C. O. Keiser used letters from local residents to help influence the decisions of their families and friends, other agents took advantage of personal recommendations to encourage immigration of ethnic communities. Important sources of these endorsements were church officials and religious journals. In a few instances priests served as agents or subagents, and church newspapers often carried land advertisements. Anders L. Mordt, the promoter of the Oslo community, invited representatives of the United Norwegian Lutheran Church to inspect his lands, knowing that their recommendations would have far-reaching effects.[33]

In practice the influence of churches extended far beyond mere recognition or approval of land ventures, for without the actual presence or explicit promise of a church building in a new community, few lots could be sold. Land developers such as W. P. Soash and T. D. Hobart willingly donated funds and land for churches.[34] Arthur P. Duggan, in his role as general manager for Littlefield Lands, actively encouraged George Washington Littlefield to contribute to the building fund for local Mennonite churches, explaining that the promise of churches was a major factor in getting the Mennonites to come. The first church built had already attracted new settlers and helped to retain others. Duggan continued, "People from Lubbock, and all over the state for that matter, have tried earnestly to switch these Mennonites . . . but the fact that they have a church at Littlefield and a community started here, has caused them to buy here."[35]

A. L. Mordt not only arranged for a church to be built at Oslo but also offered to pay $800 annually for a minimum of two years to provide for a Lutheran pastor in the area. To further strengthen Norwegian culture, and thus Norwegian interest, a school was also built and special holiday celebrations were held.[36] Since the celebrations were open to residents in surrounding communities, a two-fold purpose was met—the ethnic aspect of the community was enhanced while links were made with other neighbors.

While most of the ethnic communities remained isolated and sought to retain their folk character until after the First World War, they remained a welcome addition to the Plains. Perceived as hard-working and industrious, they qualified for acceptance. Not every group or minority was so favored. The opportunities of the Plains, so widely advertised, had definite limitations. The managers of the Double U Company, when approached about a colony of Italian immigrants, rejected the offer on the grounds that "such people arrive here in such poor condition, it is hardly thought that this proposition would be worth while."[37] In other towns boosters phrased their invitations carefully, attempting to define both the current and the future composition of their homes and defending their standards in terms of "eastern snobbery."

Among the towns with the most stringent limitations was Lubbock. As advertised by the Dillard-Powell Land Company, the town held citizens "as moral as you can find anywhere." Their brochure further emphasized that "there is not a saloon in the county; the nearest is over a hundred miles away. There is not so much as a billiard or pool room in the good town of Lubbock." Furthermore, the brochure continued, "Lubbock has three church buildings, the Methodist, Baptist and Christian, with three other organizations, the Progressive Christian Church, Episcopal and Presbyterian. At a glance you will see that we are not living in a heathen land." The real estate company's closing invitation consisted of these claims: "Come and get a home among a good class of people who are liberal, hospitable, charitable, law-abiding, and where peace and harmony abound, where there are no negroes and where you do not have to keep the door of your corn-crib and smokehouse locked, where you can leave your home and remain away for weeks at a time without fear of returning to find that a horrifying tragedy has befallen your loved ones during your absence."[38]

This community portrait was not unique to Lubbock or a single realty company. The Short and Williams booklet, advertising the upper Panhandle, echoed these sentiments by declaring, "Our population is entirely white and we are glad that this is the case; for wherever we may be, if thousands of miles from home, we know of a certainty that our loved ones are safe and can rest with the calm assurance that our families have the protection of American men."[39]

The land agents for the XIT Ranch properties not only excluded Negroes from the category of "real Americans" but also chose to deny Chinese, Japanese, and Mexicans access. These exclusions were blunt and consistent, with the preference for Anglo-Americans and those of Western European descent serving as one of the strongest controls during the land boom era.[40]

No matter how diverse the various advertisements for the Texas Plains became, the intent of the land agents was always that of attracting a specific core of settlers. A farmer did not have to be rich—indeed, the land prices were most appealing to the poorer but ambitious immigrant—but the area was not to be a haven for the homeless. The very emphasis of the land companies on selling to´ settlers rather than speculators forced agents to carefully define their potential customers.[41]

The inquiries received by the land offices came from a wide variety of locations and reflected a myriad of interests, but these same inquiries reveal a definite concentration of interest from the midwestern states and the East Texas area. During the month of July 1910 the Double U Company received letters from Forest Home, Alabama, and Duquesne, Arizona, along with three letters from cities in Missouri and three from Illinois. A few months earlier, the W. P. Soash Company reported 117 agents in Iowa working 5,886 prospects, 36 agents in Indiana with 1,988 prospects, 37 agents in Illinois with 1,821 prospects, and only 3 in Kentucky with 62 prospects among them.[42]

These patterns varied somewhat. A few companies such as the Spur Farm Lands and the Roaring Springs Townsite Company concentrated on recruiting settlers from within the state, while the others preferred to direct their efforts farther east. These patterns were maintained in the special appeals made to ethnic settlements, with some companies directing attention to South and Central Texas and others to the Midwest.[43]

No single portrait can describe the settlers who came to populate the Plains during the land boom years of 1890 to 1917. In their own words they were farmers who were "down but not out by a long sight" or recently married and "wanting to go west" or just a "good hustling man with small capital" looking for a new start. They were also "a member of the Military Band" planning for the future or a "Hardware man considered well up on this branch of business," or widows and unmarried daughters seeking to better their lives, or priests creating new communities, or even the land agents themselves, buying the land they advertised for others. Not all of the settlers who moved west stayed, for many communities were plagued by drought, and economic changes forced others to return home or move onward. Indeed, for fifteen of the fifty-one counties in the area, the population dropped between 1910 and 1920. Yet the impact of all those who came, and especially of those who stayed and encouraged others to come, truly transformed the potential of the Plains. Counties such as Collingsworth, Crosby, Floyd, Hale, Lubbock, Lynn, Potter, and Wheeler doubled and tripled their populations between the 1910 and 1920 censuses. This increase in the numbers of citizens was matched by a similar expansion in the number of farms, farm acreage, and support businesses. The changes brought by the settlers during this boom period set patterns for future growth and development that are still apparent in population and agricultural statistics.

7.

Conclusion

THE SETTLEMENT of the Texas Panhandle and South Plains area occurred in several stages. A region whose inhabitation had been limited by harsh natural conditions, it was one of the last sections of the United States to attract mass immigration. The development of such technologies as the railroads and agricultural machinery allowed settlers to alter natural patterns and to overcome the problems of adequate transportation and crop management in a semiarid climate.

The first wave of permanent settlement in the area began only after 1876 with the arrival of cattlemen and sheepherders. While the ranchers were able to control the development of the area for two decades, unforeseen changes in the national economy, the cattle market, and weather conditions soon made other uses of the land more profitable.[1] From these changes stemmed the land boom of 1890 to 1917.

Settlers had moved onto the Plains prior to 1890, entering the cattleman's domain to establish farms and trade centers, but had met with limited success. Interest in immigration and promotion grew steadily after the arrival of the railroads as local newspapers and boosters prepared advertising campaigns. Landowners and sales agents soon took advantage of this growing enthusiasm, and by 1903 land sales began in earnest.[2] The factors allowing or encouraging the opening of the Plains at this time were the development of railroads and the connections to markets, innovations in farming techniques, the decline of the cattle industry, an increased understanding of the area's agricultural possibilities, and a growing demand for new farmlands by midwestern farmers.

Yet even with these changes, settling the Panhandle and South

Plains was not a simple task. The region had long been viewed as a barren desert land, bypassed by immigrants traveling west and left to novelists' imaginations. Those involved in selling the area relied upon advertisements to overcome the old images and redefine the Plains' potential. Even though a myriad of groups and individuals were responsible for these advertisements, the information presented was remarkably uniform. There was a marked interest in attracting farmers as settlers, in developing the region as a whole even as particular sites sought preeminence, and in avoiding the dangers of speculation.

Faced with the distrust incurred by the fraudulent activities of land speculators in Kansas and Nebraska, Texas land agents sought to upgrade their own images along with those of the land through advertisements.[3] Indeed, the emphasis on the integrity and sincerity of boosters and land sellers was one of the distinguishing traits of the promotion programs for this land boom.

While the various campaigns were not without excesses and competition was often intense and occasionally vindictive, they were balanced with cooperative efforts and responsible sales terms. Typical of the local cooperative associations were those formed in Amarillo and Hereford, where real estate agents worked as "a unit in inducing immigration" and in reducing friction between agents.[4] Land companies and their representatives also participated in the development of state and national organizations that sought to improve sales techniques and public attitudes toward their lands. Anders Mordt, founder of Oslo, Texas, also helped found, in 1909, the National Dry Farming Congress, an association concerned principally with monitoring land colonization projects and promotions in the western United States.[5]

Much of the potential abuse that these organizations hoped to circumvent was avoided on the Plains through the actual sales policies of the land companies. Promoters, while adopting some of the hyperbole of their predecessors, also strove to paint an accurate picture of their properties and to attract settlers with potential to match that of the lands'. Brochures flatly stated, "We are not disposed to encourage purchase by the speculative investor" or "We will not sell land unless it is to be improved and farmed—no speculation."[6] In addition, company policies encouraged the improvement of roads and cooperation with railroads as well as assisting new farmers with appropriate crops and livestock.[7] Several companies, such as the Double U in Post and the Texas Land and Development Company in Plainview, based their sales on developed farms, providing settlers with homes, outbuildings, windmills, and

even irrigation equipment. No company completely avoided speculation, and, in fact, many of the agencies operating in the area were
themselves speculative ventures. Still, as David Gracy has observed, this activity was seldom conducted "with the intent to
defraud."[8]

Compared with the blatant excesses of the land booms in southern California in the 1880s or southern Florida in the 1920s, the
few outright frauds of West Texas seem unimaginative.[9] Most
prevalent of these schemes were railroad projects. Because these
lines were so essential to live on the Plains, plans for towns
abounded as local companies with townsites anticipated and designed communities that depended on rail access. The failure of
railways to materialize also meant the failure of the towns, and any
money invested in either was lost.

Only one enterprise, the townsite of Virginia City in Bailey
County, has been identified as a deliberate fraud. Advertisements
were based on the impending arrival of a rail line, but only a strip
of road—made to appear as the beginnings of a roadbed—was ever
built. Prospectors were also shown the lots reserved for churches
and the courthouse, but the stakes outlining these properties were
fake. The "townsite" was shown to two or three excursion groups
before being abandoned by its developers.[10]

The developers of Dominion in Lipscomb County were guilty
primarily of exaggeration in attempting to attract settlers. Their
venture proved unsuccessful; the hotel built never saw guests, and
the population of 5,000, so proudly advertised, remained a figment
of the promoters' imaginations.[11]

The majority of the deceptions that occurred on the Plains resulted more from misguided enthusiasm than from malicious intent.
Daniel Boorstin has made a careful distinction between *boosters* and
boomers, noting that "the booster was a community builder, loyal
for the time at least to his place, a true believer who cast his lot in
advance with those whom he could persuade to join him" and that
"if the booster deceived, he deceived himself along with the others."[12] From this definition, the Panhandle–South Plains was de-
cidedly a booster's frontier.

The success of the boosters and their advertisements can be attested through the amount of land sold and settled, the population
growth, the increased agricultural importance of the area, and the
continued interest in land sales after the initial boom slowed in
1917. Gracy has credited land colonizers with an essential role in
the development of the plains during this settlement phase. He has
observed that the Panhandle-Plains area would have been consid-

erably slower in developing without "assistance in locating a suitable farm, in agricultural demonstration, in erecting improvements, in adjusting notes and payments to meet the exigencies of drouth and other hardships" and that "land colonization was a primary agent, perhaps, *the* primary agent, in the settlement process, which brought the Panhandle-Plains from a cattle-grazing, frontier area to an agriculturally-based, semi-urbanized region."[13]

In numerical terms, the advertisements and promotions proved successful. The combined population of the fifty-one-county area grew from 13,787 in 1890 to 193,371 by 1920. The number of farms and corresponding amount of improved farmlands also increased dramatically, from a mere 4,131 farms representing 406,230 acres in 1900 to 14,406 farms with a total of 2,616,261 acres in 1910 to 19,385 farms and 3,669,868 acres in 1920.[14] Reading beyond the statistics, one can find a series of patterns developed during the boom years that have directed both the growth and the images of this area for the succeeding decades.

Appendix A

Population Statistics for Panhandle and South Plains
Counties, 1890–1920 and 1980

County	1890	1900	1910	1920	1980
Andrews	24	87	975	350	13,323
Armstrong	944	1,205	2,682	2,816	1,994
Bailey		4	312	517	8,168
Borden	222	776	1,386	965	859
Briscoe		1,253	2,162	2,948	2,579
Carson	356	469	2,127	3,078	6,672
Castro	9	400	1,850	1,948	10,556
Cochran		25	65	67	4,825
Collingsworth	357	1,233	5,224	9,154	4,648
Crosby	346	788	1,765	6,084	8,859
Dallam	112	146	4,001	4,528	6,531
Dawson	29	37	2,320	4,309	16,184
Deaf Smith	179	843	3,942	3,747	21,165
Dickens	295	1,151	3,092	5,876	3,539
Donley	1,056	2,756	5,284	8,035	4,075
Ector	224	381	1,178	760	115,374
Floyd	529	2,020	4,638	9,758	9,834
Gaines	68	55	1,255	1,018	13,150
Garza	14	185	1,995	4,253	5,336
Glasscock	208	286	1,143	555	1,304
Gray	203	480	3,405	4,663	26,386
Hale	721	1,680	7,566	10,104	37,590
Hall	703	1,660	8,279	11,137	5,594
Hansford	133	167	935	1,354	6,209
Hartley	252	377	1,298	1,109	3,987
Hemphill	519	815	3,170	4,280	5,304
Hockley		44	137	137	23,230
Howard	1,120	2,528	8,881	6,962	33,142
Hutchinson	58	303	892	721	26,304

County	1890	1900	1910	1920	1980
Lamb	4	31	540	1,175	18,669
Lipscomb	632	790	2,634	3,684	3,766
Loving	3	33	249	82	91
Lubbock	33	293	3,624	11,096	211,651
Lynn	24	17	1,713	4,751	8,605
Martin	264	332	1,549	1,146	4,684
Midland	1,033	1,741	3,464	2,449	82,636
Moore	15	209	561	571	16,575
Motley	139	1,257	2,396	4,107	1,950
Ochiltree	198	267	1,602	2,331	9,588
Oldham	270	349	812	709	2,283
Parmer	7	34	1,555	1,699	11,038
Potter	849	1,820	12,424	16,710	98,637
Randall	187	963	3,312	3,675	75,062
Roberts	326	620	950	1,469	1,187
Sherman	34	104	1,376	1,473	3,174
Swisher	100	1,227	4,012	4,338	9,723
Terry	21	48	1,474	2,236	14,581
Ward	77	1,451	2,389	2,615	13,976
Wheeler	778	636	5,258	7,397	7,137
Winkler	18	60	442	81	9,944
Yoakum	4	26	602	504	8,299

Source: Texas Almanac and State Industrial Guide, 1984–1985, ed. Michael T. Kingston, pp. 343–346.

Appendix B

Acres of Improved Farm Land and Number of Farms, 1900–1920

County	1900		1910		1920	
			Acres (Farms)			
Andrews	70	(12)	1,105	(18)	6,189	(57)
Armstrong	22,486	(172)	116,734	(387)	104,773	(373)
Bailey	275	(5)	11,000	(71)	13,553	(79)
Borden	3,542	(129)	25,736	(228)	24,496	(197)
Briscoe	9,434	(170)	92,418	(307)	71,923	(397)
Carson	4,663	(57)	86,357	(284)	155,793	(426)
Castro	12,131	(76)	71,235	(327)	83,029	(365)
Cochran		(1)	1,826	(16)	2,590	(14)
Collingsworth	21,474	(218)	104,892	(806)	146,179	(1,139)
Crosby	5,985	(116)	30,351	(242)	137,394	(810)
Dallam	1,280	(4)	48,443	(201)	38,645	(218)
Dawson	35	(5)	42,631	(330)	79,864	(574)
Deaf Smith	11,041	(97)	86,292	(361)	83,989	(382)
Dickens	40,842	(197)	34,504	(349)	85,703	(705)
Donley	14,504	(188)	82,008	(601)	109,411	(810)
Ector	92	(25)	4,796	(84)	10,451	(55)
Floyd	18,607	(286)	73,265	(620)	242,822	(1,289)
Gaines	55	(6)	19,717	(206)	16,103	(140)
Garza	545	(38)	16,398	(81)	49,552	(425)
Glasscock	1,100	(49)	15,384	(165)	11,125	(112)
Gray	8,782	(88)	91,759	(433)	168,645	(580)
Hale	20,313	(259)	126,514	(731)	235,880	(1,031)
Hall	25,360	(219)	117,130	(1,208)	144,160	(1,051)
Hansford	2,266	(22)	32,997	(152)	67,575	(221)
Hartley	2,641	(27)	195,052	(165)	47,570	(139)
Hemphill	11,994	(76)	52,768	(249)	77,838	(328)
Hockley	360	(5)	2,657	(23)	3,235	(18)
Howard	5,835	(130)	84,799	(819)	65,363	(422)

County	Acres (Farms) 1900		1910		1920	
Hutchinson	1,805	(65)	23,785	(150)	35,943	(134)
Lamb	370	(5)	13,797	(92)	39,687	(172)
Lipscomb	11,213	(117)	108,767	(375)	117,278	(483)
Loving		(6)	580	(79)	456	(14)
Lubbock	3,768	(46)	27,561	(208)	126,909	(1,009)
Lynn	246	(5)	20,108	(201)	87,232	(674)
Martin	203	(33)	14,414	(147)	17,195	(139)
Midland	897	(73)	16,166	(178)	14,899	(133)
Moore	1,708	(57)	21,613	(95)	20,080	(92)
Motley	8,432	(209)	36,924	(373)	62,002	(537)
Ochiltree	2,602	(71)	53,096	(264)	131,116	(336)
Oldham	11,591	(23)	12,657	(87)	28,691	(86)
Parmer	350	(1)	37,909	(161)	45,158	(212)
Potter	7,414	(79)	29,158	(162)	45,178	(166)
Randall	8,278	(96)	94,404	(363)	116,815	(383)
Roberts	3,576	(59)	18,049	(93)	44,110	(152)
Sherman	2,880	(18)	89,090	(165)	43,052	(151)
Swisher	16,210	(186)	113,052	(510)	159,879	(572)
Terry	115	(6)	23,245	(235)	32,134	(274)
Ward	5,491	(167)	17,590	(231)	19,051	(238)
Wheeler	11,889	(119)	169,254	(736)	186,329	(997)
Winkler		(12)	638	(128)	366	(27)
Yoakum	10	(1)	8,339	(107)	10,363	(109)

Source: U.S. Department of Commerce, Bureau of the Census, *Fourteenth Census of the United States, 1920: Agriculture* 6:664–686.

Appendix C

Booster Songs and Poetry

Shafter Lake
By F. L. DuPont

Fair Shafter Lake! To thee I sing
   Enchanting is the scene;
A meed to praise to thee I bring,
   Thou fairest gem serene:
The morning sun its brightness gives
   The birds their toilets make
While every breathing thing that lives
   Sings praise to Shafter Lake!

Romantic vales on every hand
   Proclaim the days gone by,
When Indian braves traversed the land
   And sought with eagle eye
The wild deer fleeing through the wood,
   Now paused his thirst to slake
The huntsman slew him where he stood
   To drink to Shafter Lake!

Long since has passed that bloody day,
   And naught but tales remain
Of savage bands on wild foray,
   And scores of settlers slain:
The wild Comanche's dreadful yell
   No more the echoes wake,
But happy homes, expressive tell
   Of peace 'round Shafter Lake!

Where once reflected from its face
   The buffalo's shaggy head.

A vision fair, of youth and grace,
  Is mirrored forth, instead:
A happy pair, with faces bright,
  Their vows of promise make,
As many sweethearts oft will plight
  Their love at Shafter Lake!

With every sort of fruit that grows
  Beneath this Western sky,
These wilds now blossom as the rose,
  Delightful to the eye:
And bounteous crops on every hand
  Slight culture do they take
Unbounded wealth stored in the land
  That lies 'round Shafter Lake!

O you, who in the city's moil,
  'Mid heat and dust you groan,
And barely live with constant toil,
  A happy home may own:
Within your reach we gladly place
  Small effort will it take
Our splendid offer quick embrace
  And come to Shafter Lake!

> Source: James Thomas Gumley, comp., *Information Concerning Shafter Lake in Andrews County*, p. 2.

In the Brazos Valley of Texas

Here's to good old Texas, boys
  Down on the Littlefield lands,
'Tis Nature's garden spot of earth,
  For here we have the land,
And rain and soil and sunshine,
  And everything so grand,
    In the Brazos Valley of Texas.

Chorus.

Hurrah, hurrah, send up a mighty cheer,
   Hurrah, hurrah, a bumper crop each year,
We've left hard winters back of us,
   And there's nothing more to fear
In the Brazos Valley of Texas.

The melons and milo maize,
   Alfalfa and the corn,
I never saw such beautiful fields
   And crops since I was born;
The apple and the peach trees,
   The verdant fields adorn
In the Brazos Valley of Texas.

The climate's mild and pleasant,
   From the Gulf the breezes blow,
The rain in season is plentiful,
   And makes the crops to grow,
We get the best of everything
   We have a mind to sow,
In the Brazos Valley of Texas.

The railroads and the schools are here,
   We make no sacrifice,
We're planting in the early spring,
   Our produce brings the price,
We're happy and contented,
   It's the farmer's paradise
In the Brazos Valley of Texas.

The richness and the depth of soil
   Make all the farmers smile.
It makes their time and money
   And their labor worth the while,
For it is as productive
   As the delta of the Nile—
In the Brazos Valley of Texas.

When autumn comes we call the dogs,
   Take down the old shotgun,
Jack rabbits, ducks and partridges
   And deer make lots of fun.
We take a team of mules for there
   Is shooting by the ton—
In the Brazos Valley of Texas.

     Source: Lamb County Leader (Littlefield, Texas), 27 June 1963, p. 4-C. Sung to the tune of "Marching through Georgia."

In the Land I Love

You ask what land I love the best,
   Littlefield Lands, my Littlefield Lands.
The fairest in the great Southwest.
   Littlefield Lands, my Littlefield Lands.
From Mother Earth a flowing stream
Of crops pours forth and fields agleam,
Fairer than any poet's dream,
   Littlefield Lands, my Littlefield Lands.

The reason why I love thee best,
   Littlefield Lands, my Littlefield Lands.
Most fertile soil in the great Southwest,
   Littlefield Lands, my Littlefield Lands.
Thy soil in forming ages old
Alluvial silt, loam rich as gold,
Enormous crop returns unfold,
   Littlefield Lands, my Littlefield Lands.

One reason why I love thee best,
   Littlefield Lands, my Littlefield Lands.
No balmier clime in the Southwest,
   Littlefield Lands, my Littlefield Lands.
To young and old abundant health
Perpetual farming brings them wealth,
Abundant crops pay as by stealth,
   Littlefield Lands, my Littlefield Lands.

Oh, land where milk and honey flow,
  Littlefield Lands, my Littlefield Lands.
Where rarest flowers in summer grow,
  Littlefield Lands, my Littlefield Lands.
Where melons and grapes and fruits do well,
Where grain and hogs and cattle tell
Me there to come and with them dwell,
  Littlefield Lands, my Littlefield Lands.

> Source: *Lamb County Leader* (Littlefield, Texas), 27 June 1963, sec. 2, p. 10. Sung to the tune of "Maryland."

[Briscoe County]

Come where the water's pure,
  Come where there's fertile soil;
Come where the crops are sure,
  Where a reward is reaped for toil.

Come where the health is good,
  Come where the people are kind;
Where noble womanhood
  Elevates and inspires the mind.

Come where the fine fruits grow,
  Come where the gardens thrive
Where the gentle zephyrs blow,
  And the people are glad they're alive.

Come where grows a small grain,
  Where the cyclones never go;
Come to the peer of the Plains,
  Procure you a home in Briscoe.

> Source: Silverton Commercial Club, *Briscoe County: Growth and Development of the Great Plains of Texas*, p. 27.

The Texas Panhandle

To the Panhandle country, my friend why not go?
  Where the winters are mild with seldom deep snow,

Where the cool breeze of summer, refreshing and grand,
  Fans the brow of the maid and laboring man.
Where water as pure as the dew drops that lie,
  And sparkle in sunlight beneath the clear sky,
Is found in abundance, and thanks to man's skill,
  Is pumped from the earth by the clever wind mill.
Where the country lies level, rich, fertile and good,
  That the rainfall is ample is well understood.
Where buffalo grass, once the friend of the beast,
  Is yielding its place to the grain of the east.
Where corn, rye, and barley, milo maize, oats and wheat,
  And fruits of the orchard, the world can not beat.
Where products of gardens, and melons compare,
  With those on exhibit at a grand country fair.
Where cattle and horses in pastures grow sleek,
  And sheep, hogs, and poultry, of them I must speak,
All are grown with profit and but little pains,
  By the farmer and ranchman of the great Texas Plains,
Where the people are prosperous and live at their ease,
  Enjoying a climate that's free from disease.
Pure air and pure water, and bright sunny skies,
  One glance at this country will open your eyes.
Where taxes are low, good laws are maintained.
  By wise legislation the country has gained
A public school fund, the envy of all
  The States in the Union, be they great or small.
Where land is now cheap, but will not so remain,
  As thousands are going on the homeseekers train.
They are buying for homes, for comfort and health,
  Advance in investments alone, will bring wealth.
My friends take advice secure a good thing,
  A home in the Panhandle is fit for a king,
But while you can, you will find out in time,
  The truth simply stated in this little rhyme.
    Source: *Hereford Brand,* 22 November 1907, p. 4.

Notes

1. Introduction

1. Lester F. Sheffy, "The Experimental Stage of Settlement in the Panhandle of Texas," *Panhandle-Plains Historical Review* 3 (1930): 100.

2. Howard Peckham, "Books and Reading on the Ohio Valley Frontier," *Mississippi Valley Historical Review* 44 (March 1958): 662–663.

3. Arnold C. Plank, "Desert versus Garden: The Role of Western Images in the Settlement of Kansas" (M.A. thesis, Kansas State University, 1962), p. 2; Frederick W. Rathjen, *The Texas Panhandle Frontier*, p. 82.

4. Walter Prescott Webb, *The Great Plains*, p. 141.

5. Richard H. Dillon, "Stephen Long's Great American Desert," *Proceedings of the American Philosophical Society* 3 (April 1967): 104; Roger L. Nichols and Patrick L. Halley, *Stephen Long and American Frontier Exploration*, pp. 167, 248; Martyn J. Bowden, "The Perception of the Western Interior of the United States, 1800–1870: A Problem in Historical Geosophy," *Proceedings of the Association of American Geographers* 1 (1969): 17. There has been some debate as to whether Long or his cartographer, Lieutenant William Swift, actually inscribed the words on the official map, but most evidence points to Long.

6. Frederic Logan Paxson, *The Last American Frontier*, p. 11.

7. Bowden, "Perception," pp. 17–19.

8. Plank, "Desert versus Garden," p. 12; Webb, *Great Plains*, p. 153.

9. John Russell Bartlett, *Personal Narrative of Explorations and Incidents in Texas, New Mexico, California, Sonora, and Chihuahua*, 1: frontispiece map.

10. John H. Tice, *Over the Plains and on the Mountains . . .* , pp. 45–46.

11. Plank, "Desert versus Garden," p. 15.

12. Charles Robert Kutzleb, "Rain Follows the Plow: The History of an Idea" (Ph.D. diss., University of Colorado, 1970), pp. 248, 260, 264, 268.

13. Ibid., pp. 269, 291.

14. U.S. Congress, House of Representatives, *Production of Rain by Artillery Firing*, House Report 786, 43d Cong., 1st sess., 1874; U.S. Congress, Senate, *Experiments in Production of Rainfall*, Senate Executive Document 45, 52d Cong., 1st sess., 1892; Mark W. Harrington, "Farwell's Rainfall Scheme," *American Meteorological Journal* 8 (June 1891): 84–91; H. A. Hazen, "Rain Making," *Scientific American* 65 (October 1891): 277.

15. John Wesley Powell, *Report on the Lands of the Arid Region of the United States, with a More Detailed Account of the Lands of Utah.*

16. U.S. Department of Agriculture, *Yearbook of Agriculture,* 1904, p. 3.

17. Texas Department of Agriculture, *The Panhandle and Llano Estacado of Texas,* by Frederick W. Mally, p. 5.

18. Ibid., p. 8.

19. L. P. Brockett, *Our Western Empire: Or the New West Beyond the Mississippi,* p. 238.

20. Ibid., pp. 82, 1124.

21. J. H. Beadle, *The Undeveloped West; or, Five Years in the Territories,* p. 51.

22. Josiah Gregg, *Commerce of the Prairies,* pp. 355, 374.

23. Richard Smith Elliott, *Notes Taken in Sixty Years,* p. 304.

24. Gene M. Gressley, *Bankers and Cattlemen,* pp. 45–46.

25. Earl Pomeroy, *In Search of the Golden West: The Tourist in Western America,* p. 68.

26. Ibid., p. 35.

27. Alfred Henry Lewis, *The Throwback: A Romance of the Southwest;* Captain Mayne Reid, *The White Chief: A Legend of North Mexico;* Frederick Holbrook, *The Dead Horseman; or Phantom Riders of Texas.*

28. Sanford E. Marovitz, "Bridging the Continent with Romantic Western Realism," in *The American Literary West,* ed. Richard W. Etulain, p. 17.

29. Ibid.

30. Henry Nash Smith, *Virgin Land: The American West as Symbol and Myth,* p. 90.

31. Ibid., pp. 176–177.

32. Caroline B. Sherman, "The Development of American Rural Fiction," *Agricultural History* 12 (January 1938): 67–76.

33. David C. Hunt, *Legacy of the West*, p. 10.

34. Keith Wheeler, *The Chroniclers*, pp. 103–134.

35. Paul Hogarth, *Artists of Horseback: The Old West in Illustrated Journalism, 1857–1900*, p. 9.

36. Wesley M. Burnside, *Maynard Dixon: Artist of the West*, p. 55.

37. Ray Stannard Baker, "The Great Southwest" *Century Magazine*, May–June 1902, p. 5.

38. Ibid., pp. 11, 13.

39. William R. Draper, "Passing of the Texas Cowboy and the Big Ranches," *Overland Monthly*, February 1905, pp. 146–150.

40. Chester T. Crowell, "Six Shooter Ethics," *The Independent*, 5 December 1912, p. 1312.

41. Robert G. Athearn, "The Great Plains in Historical Perspective," *Montana* 8 (Winter 1958): 25.

2. The Boosters

1. William C. Holden, "Immigration and Settlement in West Texas," *West Texas Historical Association Yearbook* 5 (June 1929): 72–73.

2. Garry L. Nall, "Panhandle Farming in the 'Golden Era' of American Agriculture," *Panhandle-Plains Historical Review* 46 (1973): 70; David B. Gracy, "A Preliminary Survey of Land Colonization in the Panhandle-Plains of Texas," *Museum Journal* 11 (1969): 58.

3. David M. Emmons, *Garden in the Grasslands: Boomer Literature of the Central Great Plains*, p. 64; William Curry Holden, *Alkali Trails*, pp. 77–78.

4. Daniel J. Boorstin, *The Americans: The National Experience*, pp. 127–128.

5. E. R. Archambeau, "Early Panhandle Newspapers," *Panhandle Plains Historical Review* 45 (1972): 46.

6. Roger A. Burgess, "Pioneer Quaker Farmers of the South Plains," *Panhandle-Plains Historical Review* 1 (1928): 122–123.

7. *The Stayer*, 14 August 1902.

8. *Canyon City News*, 20 November 1903, p. 1; *Randall County News*, 11 September 1908, p. 6; 24 February 1911, p. 2.

9. *Crosbyton Review*, 26 May 1916, p. 8; 2 June 1916, p. 1.

10. *Randall County News*, 1 February 1917, p. 4.
11. Boorstin, *Americans: The National Experience*, p. 125.
12. *Canyon City News*, 3 March 1905; *Hale County Herald*, 2 June 1913.
13. "The Texas Panhandle," *Hereford Brand*, 22 November 1907.
14. *Crosbyton Review*, 29 January 1909, p. 3; 22 September 1910.
15. B. R. Brunson, *The Texas Land and Development Company: A Panhandle Promotion, 1912–1956*, pp. 44–45.
16. "A Panhandle Man Tells Them about Us In Kansas City," *Daily Panhandle*, 20 October 1911, p. 2; "Regarding the Great Texas Panhandle," *Lubbock Avalanche*, 8 September 1905, p. 1.
17. *Crosby County News*, 21 January 1909; *West Texas News*, 21 August 1914.
18. *Canyon City News*, 3 April 1903, p. 2.
19. Ibid., 10 January 1908, p. 2.
20. Burgess, "Pioneer Quaker Farmers," pp. 122–123.
21. "24,198 Copies of Review," *Crosbyton Review*, 20 April 1911, p. 2.
22. *Hale County Herald*, 8 May 1913; *Dalhart Texan*, 21 May 1903; *Amarillo Herald*, 28 July 1905; *Crosbyton Review*, 1 April 1909; *Randall County News*, 3 March 1911. The *Randall County News* included not only the usual features but, apparently recognizing an interest in college sports, an entire section on local college athletes.
23. *Crosbyton Review*, 1 April 1909.
24. Ibid., 20 April 1911.
25. Dudley Morton Lynch, "Belle of the Prairie Press: A History of *The Hereford Brand*" (seminar paper, University of Texas at Austin, 1966), p. 30; *Randall County News*, 27 January 1911, p. 1; 24 March 1911, 4; *Hereford Brand* 1 September 1911, p. 1.
26. *Canyon City News*, 26 April 1907, p. 2.
27. *Crosbyton Review*, 22 April 1909; 8 September 1910; 3 November 1910; 20 April 1911; 12 January 1917.
28. *Canyon City News*, 10 April 1908; *Crosbyton Review*, 13 April 1911.
29. Lynch, "Belle of the Prairie," p. 30.
30. Seymour Connor, "The New Century," in *A History of Lubbock*, ed. Lawrence Graves, pp. 107–108; *Crosbyton Review*, 22 April 1909, p. 1.
31. *Hereford Brand*, 30 June 1911, p. 6.

32. "We Ought to Have One," *Canyon City News*, 30 March 1906, p. 2.

33. "Commercial Club Proceedings," *Canyon City News*, 29 December 1906, p. 4.

34. Amarillo Chamber of Commerce, *The Land of Promise*, p. 43.

35. Lawrence Graves, "Economic, Social, and Cultural Developments," in *A History of Lubbock*, ed. Lawrence Graves, p. 207; *Lubbock Avalanche*, 3 June 1909.

36. *Crosbyton Review*, 11 February 1911, p. 8.

37. Hereford Commercial Club, *Camera Chat from Hereford* (Hereford, Texas: Hereford Brand Print, n.d.), Land Company Brochures File, Panhandle-Plains Historical Museum, Canyon, Texas.

38. *Amarillo Daily News*, 20 October 1912, p. 9.; Young Men's Business Club of Canadian, *Canadian the Beautiful* (Wichita: Mc-Cormick-Armstrong Press, n.d.), Land Company Brochures File, Panhandle-Plains Historical Museum, Canyon, Texas.

39. *Crosbyton Review*, 15 December 1910, p. 1; *Randall County News*, 25 September 1908, p. 5.

40. *Crosbyton Review*, 25 May 1911, p. 4; *Randall County News*, 23 June 1911, p. 8; Graves, "Economic Developments," p. 207; *Amarillo Daily News*, 4 October 1912, p. 8.

41. *Canyon City News*, 27 March 1908, p. 1.

42. *Lubbock Avalanche*, 16 September 1909, pt. 2, p. 1.

3. The Railroads

1. Richard C. Overton, *Burlington West: A Colonization History of the Burlington Railroad*, p. 483.

2. Emmons, *Garden in the Grasslands*, p. 25.

3. Ibid., pp. 26–27.

4. Seymour V. Connor, "Early Land Speculation in West Texas," *Southwestern Social Science Quarterly* 42 (March 1962): 355–356; H. P. N. Gammel, ed., *The Laws of Texas, 1822–1897*, 8:989. The General Laws of Texas passed during the Fifteenth Legislature, 1876, contained "An Act to encourage the construction of railroads in Texas by the donation of lands." This act provided for sixteen sections of land for every mile of railroad completed. The land was to come from the "unappropriated public land," and the act further stated that all land acquired by rail companies was to be "alienated by said companies one-half in six years and one-

half in twelve years from the issuances of patents." Any land not sold would be forfeited to the state to once again become part of the public domain.

5. Sheffy, "The Experimental Stage of Settlement," p. 88.

6. William S. Billingsley, "The FW & DC Railroad: Giving Birth to a Line of Communities in West Texas," *Texas Humanist,* May–June 1983, pp. 16–17.

7. Laura Lynn Wyman, "The Quanah, Acme and Pacific Railway" (M.A. thesis, Midwestern University, 1967), p. v; David M. Vigness, "Transportation," in *A History of Lubbock,* ed. Lawrence Graves, pp. 393–396.

8. Missouri Pacific Railway Company, *Statistics and Information Concerning the State of Texas,* pp. 15, 33–35.

9. Ida Marie Williams Lowe, "The Role of the Railroads in the Settlement of the Texas Panhandle" (M.A. thesis, West Texas State College, 1962), p. 82; *Hereford Brand,* 8 September 1911, p. 4.

10. *The Stayer,* 4 November 1901, p. 3.

11. Richard C. Overton, *Gulf to Rockies: The Heritage of the Fort Worth and Denver–Colorado and Southern Railways, 1861–1898,* pp. 211–212.

12. Steven F. Mehls, "Garden in the Grasslands Revisited: Railroad Promotion Efforts and the Settlement of the Texas Plains," *West Texas Historical Association Yearbook* 55 (1984): 54.

13. Fort Worth and Denver City Railway, *Facts about Texas with Special Information Concerning the Panhandle,* p. 1.

14. Ibid., p 13.

15. George W. Butler, *The Farmer and the Railroad: Cooperation for Profit* (Chicago: Land and Colonization Department, Crosbyton South Plains Railroad, 1912), pp. 49–50, in Pat Brown, comp., *Land Promotion in Crosby County.*

16. Ibid., p. 29.

17. C. L. Seagraves, *Farmers Make Good in the Panhandle and South Plains of Texas;* Atchison, Topeka and Santa Fe Railway, *Panhandle and South Plains, Texas.* The college student was Ethel Trowbridge, who reported on the cotton she planted to help pay her expenses to West Texas State Normal College in Canyon.

18. Athearn, "The Great Plains," p. 22.

19. Emmons, *Garden in the Grasslands,* p. 129; Kutzleb, "Rain Follows the Plow," pp. 436–437.

20. Fort Worth and Denver City Railway, *Facts about Texas,* p. 11.

21. Missouri Pacific Railway Company, *Statistics and Information*, pp. 27–29.

22. Butler, *The Farmer and the Railroad*, p. 20.

23. Mehls, "Garden in the Grasslands Revisited," p. 53.

24. Donald E. Green, *Land of the Underground Rain: Irrigation on the Texas High Plains, 1910–1970*, pp. 166–168.

25. Butler, *The Farmer and the Railroad*, p. 24.

26. Mehls, "Garden in the Grasslands Revisited," pp. 56–57.

27. Missouri, Kansas and Texas Railway, *Texas: Empire State of the Southwest*, p. 34; Missouri Pacific Railway Company, *Statistics and Information*, p. 17; Atchison, Topeka and Santa Fe Railway, *Panhandle and South Plains*, p. 3; Butler, *The Farmer and the Railroad*, pp. 19–20.

28. Missouri Pacific Railway Company, *Statistics and Information*, pp. 78–79.

29. Butler, *The Farmer and the Railroad*, p. 29.

30. Fort Worth and Denver City Railway, *Facts about Texas*, pp. 9–10.

31. Louva Myrtis Douglas, "The History of the Agricultural Fairs of Texas" (M.A. thesis, University of Texas at Austin, 1943), p. 36; Nall, "The Farmers' Frontier," p. 7; Holden, "Immigration and Settlement," p. 86.

32. *Crosbyton Review*, 25 May 1911, p. 4.

33. "Cheap Rates to the Panhandle," *Canyon City News*, 3 October 1903, p. 1.

34. Mehls, "Garden in the Grasslands Revisited," p. 60; A. A. Glisson to D. B. Keeler, 28 July 1910, FF4123, and D. B. Keeler to C. Adair, 18 November 1914, FF310, Fort Worth and Denver City Railroad, Records [microfilm], Southwest Collection, Texas Tech University, Lubbock.

35. *Plainview Evening Herald*, 2 June 1914, p. 6.

36. Billingsley, "FW & DC," p. 18.

37. Gracy, "A Preliminary Survey," p. 67.

38. *Hereford Brand*, 28 September 1916, p. 3.

39. Billingsley, "FW & DC," p. 18.

40. *Canyon City News*, 6 November 1903, p. 3; 4 August 1905, p. 2; *Dalhart Texan*, 24 September 1915, p. 4.

41. Nall, "Panhandle Farming," p. 74.

42. Theodore Dreiser, "The Railroad and the People: A New Educational Policy Now Operating in the West," *Harper's New Monthly Magazine*, February 1900, p. 79.

43. Seagraves, *Farmers Make Good*, p. 1.

44. "Santa Fe Farm Train Here," *Hereford Brand,* 24 February 1911, p. 1.

45. Seagraves, *Farmers Make Good,* p. 2; Billingsley, "FW & DC," p. 16; Lowe, "The Role of the Railroads," p. 82; Texas Agricultural Experiment Station, *A History of Small Grain Crops in Texas: Wheat, Oats, Barley, Rye, 1582–1976,* by Irvin M. Atkins, p. 12.

46. The Campbell method of dryland farming was basically a tillage system designed to help maintain moisture in the soil. The system combined plowing, packing, and harrowing of fields and the use of summer tillage over summer fallow.

47. *Reeves County Record,* 1 December 1911, p. 2.

48. "It Means Much," *Canyon City News,* 13 November 1903, p. 2.

4. The Ranchers

1. Examples of novels written since the 1920s using farmer-rancher conflict as a theme include Clarence E. Mulford, *Hopalong Cassidy Returns* (1923; reprint, New York: Aeonian Press, 1974); Loula Grace Erdman, *The Edge of Time* (New York: Dodd, Mead, 1950); Clifton Adams, *Reckless Men* (Garden City, N.Y.: Doubleday, 1962); Brett Austin, *Sagebrush Saga* (New York: Avalon, 1969); Jane Gilmore Rushing, *Tamzen* (Garden City, N.Y.: Doubleday, 1972). Two of the authors, Erdman and Rushing, have direct ties to the Panhandle area. Gracy, "A Preliminary Survey," p. 61.

2. R. D. Holt, "Texas Had Hot County Elections," *West Texas Historical Association Yearbook* 24 (October 1948): 20.

3. Roger A. Burgess, "The History of Crosby County" (M.A. thesis, University of Texas at Austin, 1927), pp. 85–87; Burgess, "Pioneer Quaker Farmers," p. 117; Nellie Witt Spikes and Temple Ann Ellis, *Through the Years: A History of Crosby County, Texas,* pp. 35–36; Hank Smith, "Along down the Reminiscent Line," *Crosbyton Review,* 29 February 1912, p. 4. The area cowboys also discouraged continued settlement by Quakers through marriage. Apparently too many Quaker daughters left to marry cowboys, and concerned parents began moving away.

4. Gammel, ed., *The Laws of Texas,* 10: 794–795, 1238–1242. These laws increased the amount of land one individual could purchase and required that land be offered for sale before releasing. If the land was not purchased, the original leasee could release it.

5. David J. Murrah, *C. C. Slaughter: Rancher, Banker, Baptist,* p. 104; *Ketner v. Rogan,* 68 *Southwestern Reporter* (Tex.), 775 (1902).

6. J. A. Rickard, "South Plains Land Rushes," *Panhandle-Plains Historical Review* 2 (1929): 98–99.

7. Rickard, "South Plains," pp. 99–102; Murrah, *C. C. Slaughter,* pp. 107–109.

8. Mr. and Mrs. M. G. Abernathy to Ike Connor, 3–4 June 1956, Oral History Interview, Southwest Collection, Texas Tech University; Seymour V. Connor, ed., *Builders of the Southwest,* pp. 4–5; David Murrah, "From Ranching to Dry Farming" (Paper presented at the Sam Blair Lecture Series, South Plains College, Levelland, Texas, 28 October 1983).

9. Mary A. Blankenship, *The West Is for Us: The Reminiscences of Mary A. Blankenship,* ed. Seymour V. Connor, pp. 42–43.

10. J. Evetts Haley, *Charles Goodnight: Cowman and Plainsman,* pp. 382–383. Goodnight has also been credited with planting one of the first crops of wheat in the Panhandle. See Texas Agricultural Experiment Station, *The History of Small Grain Crops in Texas,* p. 11.

11. Lester F. Sheffy, *Francklyn Land and Cattle Company,* p. 259.

12. Ibid., pp. 261–262.

13. Murrah, *C. C. Slaughter,* p. 115. Apparently relations between the two men were cordial, even though Soash portrayed himself as having bested the cattle kings of Texas in obtaining their lands. This claim was possibly the closest Soash ever came to misrepresenting the Slaughter Lands. "Selling Texas Land at Retail: Success of the W. P. Soash Land Company Due to Advertising," *Judicious Advertising and Advertising Experience,* July 1908, pp. 25–27.

14. Gary L. Nall, "The Farmers' Frontier," p. 4; Wyman, "The Quanah, Acme and Pacific Railway," pp. 67–68.

15. Sheffy, *Francklyn,* p. 290.

16. George Tyng to Frederick de P. Foster, 21 February 1902, Francklyn Land and Cattle Company, Records, 1882–1957, Panhandle-Plains Historical Museum, Canyon, Texas. This collection will be referred to hereafter as Francklyn, PPHM.

17. Charles Jones to Frank Hastings, 3 April 1908, Espuela Land and Cattle Company, Records, 1900–1908, Correspondence Book 3, Southwest Collection, Texas Tech University, Lubbock. This collection will be referred to hereafter as Espuela, SWC.

18. Charles Jones to S. M. Swenson and Sons, 18 August

1908, Espuela, Correspondence Book 3, SWC; J. E. Ericson, "Colonization of the Spur Farm Lands," *West Texas Historical Association Yearbook* 31 (October 1955): 49.

19. Murrah, C. C. *Slaughter*, pp. 110–115.

20. David B. Gracy, *The Littlefield Lands: Colonization on the Texas Plains, 1912–1920*, pp. 13–14, 30–31, 36.

21. William M. Pearce, *The Matador Land and Cattle Company*, p. 138.

22. Statement—Acreage Property Sold to October 31, 1914, Exhibit B; Report from Charles Sommer, 23 December 1916; Loss and Gain Account, 30 January 1918; Charles Sommer to John MacBain, 18 September 1915; Charles Sommer to John MacBain, 26 November 1915, Matador Land and Cattle Company, Records, 1881–1952, Roaring Springs Townsite Company, Southwest Collection, Texas Tech University, Lubbock. This collection will be referred to hereafter as Matador, Roaring Springs, SWC. Somewhat surprising in light of the Matador's contributions to Roaring Springs is the fact that the brochure contains no reference to the ranch.

23. Mr. Black's Report on General Conditions, 1 December 1915; Charles Sommer to John MacBain, 21 April 1915; Charles Sommer to John MacBain, 7 July 1915; Charles Sommer to John MacBain, 8 January 1919, Matador, Roaring Springs, SWC.

24. CB Live Stock Company, *Why Choose Crosby County, Texas for Farming* (Crosbyton: CB Live Stock Company, [1912]); "Its Past and Present, Crosbyton, Crosby County, Texas," *Crosbyton Review*, 29 February 1912.

25. The Francklyn Land and Cattle Company failed as a ranching enterprise in 1886 and came under the trusteeship of Frederick de P. Foster and Cornelius Cuyler. Under their direction the ranch was managed as leased pasture lands under the name White Deer Lands until colonization became feasible.

26. George Tyng to Frederick Foster, 5 March 1903, Francklyn, PPHM.

27. George Tyng to Frederick Foster, 21 February 1902, Francklyn, PPHM.

28. George Tyng to Frederick Foster, 5 March 1903, Francklyn, PPHM.

29. Lester F. Sheffy, *The Life and Times of Timothy Dwight Hobart, 1855–1935*, pp. 194–195; George Tyng to Frederick Foster, 26 April 1902; George Tyng to Frederick Foster, 5 March 1903; T. D. Hobart to Frederick Foster, 18 March 1908, Francklyn, PPHM.

30. Sheffy, *Life and Times of Hobart,* pp. 194–195; T. D. Hobart to Frederick Foster, 23 March 1908 and 13 May 1908, Francklyn, PPHM. Tyng also addressed the idea of a hotel in his letter of 5 March 1903 and offered perhaps his most practical advice in noting that the wallpaper selected "should be strong, pretty and cheap. Patterns to reflect light as much as possible without too gaudily displaying dirt, tobacco juice etc."

31. David B. Gracy, "Arthur P. Duggan and the Early Development of Littlefield," *West Texas Historical Association Yearbook* 44 (October 1968): 45.

32. Arthur Duggan to George Littlefield, 16 May 1916 and 30 December 1916, George Washington Littlefield Papers, 1860–1919, Eugene C. Barker Texas History Center, University of Texas at Austin. This collection will be referred to hereafter as Littlefield, Barker.

33. *Littlefield News,* 12 December 1912; Gracy, *The Littlefield Lands,* pp. 14, 31.

34. Charles Jones to S. M. Swenson and Sons, 4 July 1908, 11 July 1908, and 14 December 1908, Espuela, Correspondence Book 3, SWC. Although Jones encouraged donations to several groups, he did express reservations about the Baptists. Writing to Frank Hastings on 12 March 1908, he noted, "On general principles I am not inclined to encourage the Baptists: They want to use our tanks in summer and it seems a little heartless to insist that the converts stand in a [dipping] pen to reclaim absorbed water, but their faith is not in keeping with the conditions of the country."

35. Charles Jones to T. M. Richardson, 29 December 1908, Espuela, Correspondence Book 3, SWC; 1905 Annual Report, 1908 Annual Report, 1915 Annual Report, XIT Ranch Records, 1886–1915, Panhandle-Plains Historical Museum, Canyon (this collection will be referred to hereafter as XIT Ranch, PPHM); *Nara Visa News,* July 1907, Henry Bradley Sanborn Papers, 1896–1950, Panhandle-Plains Historical Museum, Canyon; Seymour V. Connor, "The Founding of Lubbock," in *A History of Lubbock,* ed. Lawrence Graves, pp. 74–75.

36. The Henry B. Sanborn Papers in the Panhandle-Plains Historical Museum, Canyon, contain excellent examples of these offers.

37. Annual Report to Right Honorable the Marquis of Tweedale, 31 October 1886, XIT Ranch, PPHM.

38. 1889, 1896, 1899, and 1901 Annual Reports; Boyce to A. Taylor, 10 January 1890, XIT Ranch, PPHM.

39. 1892 Annual Report, XIT Ranch, PPHM.

40. *Dalhart Texan,* 4 November 1905, p. 1.

41. John J. Burns to George Findlay, 11 December 1905, XIT Ranch, PPHM.

42. Charles Jones to Commissioner of Agriculture, 7 November 1908; Charles Jones to Thomas Tobin, 2 December 1908; Charles Jones to Baker Bros., 28 October 1908, Espuela, Correspondence Book 3, SWC.

43. Charles Jones to S. M. Swenson and Sons, 7 December 1908, Espuela, Correspondence Book 3, SWC; Texas Agricultural Experiment Station, *Report of the Director on the Establishment of the New State Stations,* by H. H. Harrington, p. 5. One of Spur's competitors for the station was Amarillo. While Amarillo failed to get a station in 1909, Henry Sanborn, owner of the Bravo Ranch, continued to work for a station for the Amarillo area.

44. Gracy, *The Littlefield Lands,* pp. 18, 27–28, 70–71.

45. Sheffy, *Life and Times of Hobart,* pp. 116, 186–190.

46. J. Evetts Haley, *The XIT Ranch of Texas and the Early Days of the Llano Estacado,* pp. 220–221; Frank H. Hayne, "Early Days in Parmer County," *West Texas Historical Association Yearbook* 23 (October 1947): 28; John H. Wills to George Findlay, 16 May 1905; John Burns Land and Cattle Company to George Findlay, 8 November 1905; George Findlay to Wm. Nicholson, 24 May 1905; George Findlay to John Sebastian, 24 May 1905, XIT Ranch, PPHM.

47. "Prizes at Great Corn Show," *The Bulletin* [of the Chicago Association of Commerce], 5 July 1907, p. 1.

48. Eli Browning to Sanborn and Nelson, 3 July 1907, 7 October 1907; Ralston to Sanborn and Nelson, 8 April 1907; R. S. Chamberlain to Sanborn and Nelson, 22 November 1907, Henry Bradley Sanborn Papers, 1896–1950, Panhandle-Plains Historical Museum, Canyon. This collection will be referred to hereafter as Sanborn, PPHM.

49. Rawlings to George Littlefield, 3 March 1914; Advertising Account Ledger, 1912–1915; Arthur Duggan to George Littlefield, 20 February 1914, 1 May 1914, Littlefield, Barker; Gracy, *The Littlefield Lands,* pp. 48–50.

50. Nall, "Panhandle Farming," pp. 70–71; Charles Jones to W. A. Field, 14 December 1908, Espuela, Correspondence Book 4, SWC; Clifford B. Jones to David Gracy, 28 February 1968, Oral History Interview, Southwest Collection, Texas Tech University, Lubbock.

51. Charles Jones to Frank Hastings, 21 May 1908, Charles

Jones to S. M. Swenson and Sons, 18 April 1908, Espuela, Correspondence Book 3, SWC.

52. Charles Jones to S. M. Swenson and Sons, 17 April 1908; 19 July 1908, Espuela, Correspondence Book 3, SWC.

53. T. D. Hobart, *White Deer Lands in the Panhandle of Texas*; Charles Jones to S. M. Swenson and Sons, 25 December 1908, Espuela, Correspondence Book 3 SWC.

54. Arthur P. Duggan to George Littlefield, 28 April 1917, Littlefield, Barker.

55. Arthur P. Duggan to Barry Johnson, 17 May 1913, Littlefield, Barker; Gracy, *The Littlefield Lands*, p. 18.

56. Haley, *The XIT Ranch*, pp. 223–224; Clifford B. Jones to David C. Gracy, 27 March 1968, Oral History Interview, Southwest Collection, Texas Tech University, Lubbock.

57. T. D. Hobart to Frederick Foster, 19 January 1906, Francklyn, PPHM; Arthur P. Duggan to George Littlefield, 16 February 1916, Littlefield, Barker; Gracy, "Arthur P. Duggan," p. 44; Haley, *The XIT Ranch*, pp. 223–224.

5. Land Agents and Colonizers

1. Gracy, "A Preliminary Survey," p. 66; Donald Green, "The Speculator as a Promoter and Developer of Irrigation on the Texas High Plains, 1910–1920," *West Texas Historical Association Yearbook* 46 (1970): 189–190.

2. Harry S. Walker, "Economic Development of Lubbock," in *A History of Lubbock*, ed. Lawrence Graves, p. 302; *Dalhart Texan*, 10 November 1906, pp. 1, 8.

3. Gracy, *The Littlefield Lands*, p. 43.

4. See letterheads for T. E. Waggoner to Knoblauch Land Company, 11 February 1908; C. Z. Armstrong to H. B. Sanborn, 22 March 1909; R. J. Becker to Sanborn and Nelson, 3 August 1907, Sanborn, PPHM, and Texas Nebraska Land Company advertisement, *Crosbyton Review*, 25 February 1909, p. 3.

5. R. S. Bayne to H. B. Sanborn, 9 April 1909; Cora E. Cherry to H. B. Sanborn, 4 October 1909, Sanborn, PPHM.

6. Thelma Stevens, "History of Bailey County" (M.A. thesis, Texas Technological College, 1939), pp. 45–48.

7. C. S. Treadwell to Sanborn and Nelson, 23 October 1907, Sanborn, PPHM.

8. M. V. Kelly to H. B. Sanborn, 10 February 1909, 22 July 1909; H. H. Anderson to H. B. Sanborn, 11 December 1908, Sanborn, PPHM.

9. Contract, South and West Land Company and Wither-spoon and Gough, 20 July 1905, L. Gough Collection, Interview File, Panhandle-Plains Historical Museum, Canyon.

10. South and West Land Company, *The Last of the Great Prairie Farming Lands*, pp. 9, 10, 14.

11. *Des Moines* (Iowa) *Register and Leader*, 12 June 1909, p. 11.

12. L. K. Lee to L. G. Conner, 5 March 1915, Lincoln Guy Conner Collection, Panhandle-Plains Historical Museum, Canyon. Lee's offer was also interesting because of its format. He used a form letter with appropriate blank spaces for adding a few personal touches.

13. A. L. Rasmusen to Sanborn and Nelson, 15 January 1908, Sanborn, PPHM.

14. *Crosbyton Review*, 14 September 1911, p. 8.

15. Ibid., 11 March 1909, p. 7.

16. *Canyon City News*, 10 November 1905, p. 4.

17. Broadside, "O'Keefe Ranch," Ansley Realty Company, Lincoln Guy Conner Collection, Panhandle-Plains Historical Museum, Canyon.

18. Short and Williams Real Estate Company, *Land in the Panhandle of Texas*, pp. 13–14.

19. Green, "Speculator as Promoter," pp. 189–190; D. L. McDonald, *Where Crops Never Fail; Hereford Brand*, 20 January 1911, p. 2.

20. Green, "Speculator as Promoter," pp. 191–194; *Hale County Herald*, 30 January 1913, p. 3.

21. Gracy, "A Preliminary Survey," p. 70.

22. Federal Writer's Project Material, "Notes on Deaf Smith County," 2–3 April, 1936, pp. 6–8, typescript, William Pulver Soash Papers, 1906–1959, Southwest Collection, Texas Tech University, Lubbock. Hereafter referred to as Soash Papers, SWC.

23. Don Casey, "The Early History of Shallowater," *Museum Journal* 12 (1970): 124.

24. Gracy, "A Preliminary Survey," pp. 72–73; Roysten E. Willis, "Ghost Towns of the South Plains" (M.A. thesis, Texas Technological College, 1941), p. 69; Federal Writer's Project Material, "Notes on Deaf Smith County," pp. 3–4, Soash Papers, SWC.

25. Stratton Land Company, *Invest a Few Dollars in a New Town*, Porterville, Texas, Reference File, Southwest Collection, Texas Tech University, Lubbock.

26. Ibid.

27. Olton Townsite Company, *We Wish to Tell You of the New County Seat 'Olton'*, Soash Papers, SWC.

28. *Dalhart Texan*, 11 April 1913, p. 5.

29. Ibid., 30 April 1903, p. 8.

30. Kyle M. Buckner, "History of Brownfield, Texas" (M.A. thesis, Texas Technological College, 1943), pp. 24–29.

31. C. O. Keiser to Supt. Cap E. Miller, 4 August 1906; C. O. Keiser to F. A. Miller, 8 December 1906; C. O. Keiser to Louis Bronellate, 2 January 1907, C. O. Keiser Papers, Panhandle-Plains Historical Museum, Canyon (hereafter referred to as Keiser, PPHM); William M. Black and Lowell H. Harrison, "C. O. Keiser and the Farmers' Settlement of Randall County," *Panhandle-Plains Historical Review* 43 (1970): 60–64; William M. Black, "C. O. Keiser's Economic Activities in Randall County, Texas" (M.A. thesis, West Texas State University, 1960), p. 82.

32. Crosby County Historical Commission, *A History of Crosby County, 1876–1977*, p. 157; Spikes and Ellis, *Through the Years*, p. 412.

33. Crosby County Historical Commission, *A History of Crosby County*, p. 157. Bassett's fame spread beyond the Crosby County area; he was the subject of another praise-filled article in the *Fort Worth Star-Telegram*, 25 November 1913.

34. *Crosbyton Review*, 29 February 1912.

35. Butler, *The Farmer and the Railroad*; Bassett Land and Live Stock Company, *Three Ages of Crosby County: A Land of Health, Comfort and Prosperity*; CB Live Stock Company, *Why Choose Crosby County, Texas*; all in Brown, *Land Promotion in Crosby County*.

36. Butler, *The Farmer and the Railroad*, p. 16.

37. *Canyon News*, 4 January 1907, p. 1.

38. Lois Bassett Carpenter to Pat Brown, 25 November 1983, Oral History Interview, Southwest Collection, Texas Tech University, Lubbock; Crosby County Historical Commission, *A History of Crosby County*, p. 157.

39. Texas Land and Development Company to Samuel W. Sawyer, 17 January 1917; Texas Land and Development Company to B. W. Palmer, 26 November 1914; Texas Prairie Lands, Limited, General Circular, February 1917, Texas Land and Development Company Records, 1912–1955, Southwest Collection, Texas Tech University, Lubbock (hereafter referred to as TLD); Green, "Speculator as Promoter," p. 194.

40. Texas Prairie Lands, Limited, General Circular, 1917, TLD, p. 1.

41. Brunson, *The Texas Land and Development Company*, p. 5.

42. Draft of Contract, Texas Land and Development Company and M. D. Henderson, 1913, TLD.

43. Texas Land and Development Company, Trustees, J. H. Slaton and H. C. Randolph, Development Expenditures to February 28, 1913, TLD.

44. Brunson, *The Texas Land and Development Company*, pp. 44–45. Many citizens supported this company to the extent that they actively discouraged local agents from competing on land sales.

45. Brunson, *The Texas Land and Development Company*, pp. 46–50; Victor Wallen to E. Dowden, 1 December 1915, TLD.

46. Brunson, *The Texas Land and Development Company*, p. 51; R. S. Charles to B. R. Brunson, 14 September 1959, Billy Ray Brunson Papers, 1918–1960, Southwest Collection, Texas Tech University, Lubbock.

47. C. E. Craig to F. A. Kendall, 21 January 1918; Texas Prairie Lands, Limited, General Circular, 1917, TLD; Brunson, *The Texas Land and Development Company*, pp. 55–57.

48. Post experimented for a number of years with the idea of causing rainfall through the discharge of dynamite. This idea was based on research on unusual weather conditions following military campaigns. Records in the Double U Company Records in the Southwest Collection indicate that Post was quite unsuccessful in this project.

49. H. C. Hawk to Calvin Roberts, 12 February 1907, Double U Company Records, 1907–1923, Southwest Collection, Texas Tech University, Lubbock. Hereafter referred to as Double U.

50. S. B. Bardwell to C. W. Post, 5 November 1911; H. C. Hawk to Double U Company, 11 November 1913, Double U.

51. W. O. Stevens to H. C. Hawk, 8 April 1914; S. B. Bardwell to Albert MacRae, 17 September 1913; S. B. Bardwell to John B. Joseph, 26 March 1913; Arthur Williams to Double U Company, 16 February 1914, Double U; Charles Dudley Eaves and C. A. Hutchinson, *Post City, Texas: C. W. Post's Colonizing Activities in West Texas*, p. 115. Not surprisingly this booklet did not meet Double U standards; see S. B. Bardwell to C. W. Post, 29 January 1914.

52. Eaves and Hutchinson, *Post City*, pp. 92, 117, 129; H. M. Bainer to W. O. Stevens, 15 November 1912; Arthur Williams to Double U Company, 13 April 1914; Double U Company to *Crosbyton Review*, 8 January 1912; Double U Company to *Lubbock Avalanche*, 8 January 1912, Double U.

53. Quoted in Eaves and Hutchinson, *Post City*, p. 93.

54. Eaves and Hutchinson, *Post City*, pp. 66–67; S. B. Bardwell to Mrs. E. K. Thompson, 20 April 1914; S. B. Bardwell to T. R. Walker, 5 August 1913; H. C. Hawk to J. F. Hartford, 16 October 1915; typescript newspaper write-up, 5 January 1912, Double U.

55. A. B. Williams to Double U Company, 19 March 1914, Double U.

56. C. L. Seagraves to H. C. Hawk, 9 January 1914; 13 January 1914; S. B. Bardwell to A. B. Williams, 19 December 1913, Double U.

57. Soash was one of the agents the Double U Company attempted to recruit in 1913. He apparently met their high standards but was then involved with land sales in Crosby County. He was selling lands for John Ralls, a competitor of Julien Bassett. See correspondence between S. B. Bardwell and W. P. Soash, 31 December 1913 through 27 January 1914, Double U.

58. Laura V. Hamner, interview with W. P. Soash, Federal Writer's Project, 15 November 1936, Mrs. David C. Gracy Papers, 1845–1951, Southwest Collection, Texas Tech University, Lubbock.

59. "Selling Texas Land at Retail," *Judicious Advertising and Advertising Experience*, July 1908, pp. 24–28.

60. David B. Gracy, "Selling the Future: A Biography of William Pulver Soash," *Panhandle-Plains Historical Review* 50 (1977): 17.

61. Expenditures of W. P. Soash Land Company, 1909–1916, Soash Papers, SWC.

62. Laura V. Hamner, interview with W. P. Soash, Federal Writer's Project, pp. 1–3.

63. W. P. Soash Land Company, *The Big Springs Country of Texas*, p. 42.

64. Laura V. Hamner, interview with W. P. Soash, Federal Writer's Project, p. 1.

6. The Settlers

1. Paul W. Gates, "The Role of the Land Speculator in Western Development," in *Public Lands: Studies in the History of the Public Domain*, ed. Vernon Carstensen, p. 350.

2. Typescript, "Mr. and Mrs. Michael Mertels," Mrs. John W. Naylor Papers, James R. Record Collection of West Texas Pioneers, 1936–1959, Southwest Collection, Texas Tech University, Lubbock.

3. John D. Hicks, "The Western-Middle West, 1900–1914," *Agricultural History* 20 (April 1946): 73–75; Peter L. Petersen, "A New Oslo on the Plains: The Anders L. Mordt Land Company and Norwegian Migration to the Texas Panhandle," *Panhandle-Plains Historical Review* 49 (1976): 28; Nall, "Panhandle Farming," p. 76.

4. Moody Land Company, *Moody Farm Lands*, p. 5.

5. *Spur Farm Lands*, p. 12.

6. Petersen, "A New Oslo," p. 28.

7. W. R. Howard to [Double U Company], 7 April 1910; Mr. A. Fairchild to C. W. Post, 24 June 1913; Mrs. Lizzie Kingsbury to C. W. Post. 18 July 1910, Double U.

8. Mr. Black's Report on General Conditions, 1 December 1915, Matador, SWC.

9. Charles Jones to S. M. Swenson and Sons, 25 August 1908, Espuela, Correspondence Book 3, SWC.

10. Dillard-Powell Land Company, *Lubbock, Lubbock County: The Best Cheap Lands in the Southwest for Diversified Farming*, p. 27.

11. Robert Leslie Martin, "The City Moves West: Economic and Industrial Growth of the Southern Llano Estacado" (Ph.D. diss., University of Oklahoma, 1959), p. 28.

12. Black, "C. O. Keiser's Economic Activities," pp. 48–49.

13. W. P. Soash Land Company, *Big Springs Country of Texas*, p. 44.

14. *Des Moines Register and Leader*, 12 November 1909, p. 11.

15. Black and Harrison, "C. O. Keiser," p. 63.

16. Mrs. C. M. Roberts to Post City Land Company, 4 August 1913; Mrs. W. A. Riggs to Double U Company, 3 August 1910, Double U.

17. Bertha Ingalls to C. W. Post, 22 September 1909, Double U. In their response of 29 September 1909, the Double U officials encouraged her to visit and even gave explicit travel instructions.

18. See the correspondence files of the Double U Company Records, Southwest Collection, especially Sara Park to C. W. Post, 14 February 1908; Linnie Price to C. W. Post, 26 July 1910; Mrs. L. A. Mason to L. M. Brown, 4 February 1909; R. L. Lorenz to Double U Company, 25 November 1909, 11 January 1910; and Mrs. Hattie Ingram to Double U Company, 30 April 1914.

19. Billy M. Jones, *Health-Seekers in the Southwest, 1817–1900*, pp. 65, 103.

20. *Texas Almanac and State Industrial Guide*, 1910, p. 11; Jones, *Health-Seekers*, p. 104.

21. Jones, *Health-Seekers*, p. 110; Evans and Hutchinson, *Post City*, p. 5.

22. W. A. King to C. W. Post, 21 February 1908; Dr. G. M. Shropsire to Double U Company, 7 January 1915; Jno. L. Lipe to C. W. Post, 25 January 1909; and Peter Hirschy to C. W. Post, 20 March 1913, Double U.

23. Dillard-Powell Land Company, *Lubbock, Lubbock County*, p. 16.

24. Rawlings-Knapp Realty Company, *Littlefield Lands: The Best Farm Lands*, p. 6.

25. The first settlements on the Texas Plains have been identified as the Methodist colony at Clarendon and the Quaker community of Estacado. See Gracy, "A Preliminary Survey," p. 62.

26. Hubert Wilhelm Oppe, "Umbarger: Its History and People: A Monograph on a German Settlement in the Texas Panhandle," Canyon, Texas, June 1964, mimeographed, pp. 13–14; Rawlings-Knapp Realty Company, *Littlefield Lands*, p. 2; Gracy, "Selling the Future," p. 23; Victor Wallen to E. Dowden, 1 December 1915, TLD; T. D. Hobart to F. Foster, 22 April 1911, Francklyn, PPHM.

27. Oppe, "Umbarger," pp. 14–15.

28. Rawlings-Knapp Realty Company, *Littlefield Lands*, p. 2.

29. T. Lindsay Baker, "The White Deer Polish Colony," *Panhandle-Plains Historical Review* 56 (1983): 24; Petersen, "A New Oslo," pp. 28–29, 33; Bobby D. Weaver, "Father Joseph Reisdorff: Catholic Colonizer of the Plains," *Panhandle-Plains Historical Review* 56 (1983): 135–136; Rudolph Horn to Samuel Bardwell, 10 December 1913, Double U.

30. Weaver, "Father Joseph," p. 138; Gracy, *The Littlefield Lands*, p. 47.

31. Victor Wallen to E. Dowden, 1 December 1915, TLD.

32. Charles P. Flanagin, "The Origins of Nazareth, Texas" (M.A. thesis, West Texas State Teachers College, 1948), pp. 20–23; Peter L. Petersen, "Patterns in Assimilation: Two German-Lutheran Congregations in the Texas Panhandle," *Panhandle-Plains Historical Review* 56 (1983): 105–106; Baker, "White Deer," p. 22.

33. Petersen, "A New Oslo," p. 30.

34. Baker, "White Deer," p. 29; Laura V. Hamner, interview with W. P. Soash, Federal Writer's Project, p. 4. Soash contributed to the church in Lyola, a town he founded in conjunction with I. R. Unterbrink for a German Catholic colony. This town proved less successful than the Polish colony at White Deer, which was aided by T. D. Hobart, due primarily to a drought in the Lyola area.

35. Arthur P. Duggan to G. W. Littlefield, 39 December 1916, Littlefield, Barker.

36. Petersen, "A New Oslo," pp. 29–30, 33.

37. Eaves and Hutchinson, *Post City*, p. 149.
38. Dillard-Powell Land Company, *Lubbock, Lubbock County*, p. 42.
39. Short and Williams Real Estate Company, *Land in the Panhandle*, p. 11.
40. *Reservation Lands: 500,000 Acres Offered for Sale as Farm Homes* (N.p., n.d.), Land Company Brochures File, PPHM; see also Butler, *The Farmer and the Railroad*, p. 5; Knoblauch Land Company, "Flyer for Bravo Ranch," Sanborn, PPHM; Olton Townsite Company, *We Wish to Tell You*, p. 9; Farwell Development Company, *Farwell, Texas* (Chicago, n.d.), Land Company Brochures File, PPHM.
41. In the case of the Double U Company, very specific guidelines were prescribed for agents. A. B. Williams, general counsel for C. W. Post, wrote to the company in a letter dated 14 March 1914, "Only renters or small farmers who have a thousand dollars or upward should be talked to. Time should not be spent with any of the others. The man of means should not be talked to because he would only buy to speculate; he would not buy to go there and live. What we want is actual, bonafide settlers."
42. Double U Company Records, Correspondence File, 1909–1910, Double U; "Summary of Prospects Submitted by Agents," 17 September 1909, Soash Papers, SWC.
43. Clifford B. Jones to David B. Gracy, 28 February 1968, Oral History Interview, Southwest Collection, Texas Tech University, Lubbock; Charles Somner to Mr. Macbain, 22 June 1916, Matador, Roaring Springs, SWC; Dianna Everett and Cathey Kelly, "First You Work: Germans from Russia to Texas," *Panhandle-Plains Historical Review* 56 (1983): 77–78; Petersen, "Patterns of Assimilation," p. 108; Meredith McClain and Judy Harrell, "The Persistence and Change of Ethnicity: A Study of the German-Catholic Community of Nazareth, Texas," *Panhandle-Plains Historical Review* 56 (1983): 143; Terry G. Jordan, "The German Settlement of Texas after 1865," *Southwestern Historical Quarterly* 73 (October 1969): 205.

7. Conclusion

1. Jayme A. Sokolow, "The Demography of a Ranching Frontier: The Texas Panhandle in 1880," *Panhandle-Plains Historical Review* 55 (1982): 78–79; Rathjen, *The Texas Panhandle Frontier*, p. 229.
2. Gracy, "A Preliminary Survey," pp. 64–66.

3. Gracy, "Selling the Future," p. 25.

4. "Amarillo Land Men Organize," *Canyon City News*, 3 February 1905, p. 2; "Special Trains for Hereford," ibid., 17 January 1908, p. 2.

5. Petersen, "A New Oslo," p. 36; "To Encourage Immigration," *Dalhart Texan*, 21 February 1913, p. 1.

6. Eaves and Hutchinson, *Post City*, p. 154; *Spur Farm Lands*, pp. 26–27.

7. Charles Sommer to John McBain, 21 November 1916, Matador, Roaring Springs, SWC; Charles Jones to S. M. Swenson and Sons, 25 December 1908, Espuela, SWC; Garry Lynn Nall, "Agricultural History of the Texas Panhandle, 1880–1965" (Ph.D. diss., University of Oklahoma, 1972), p. 41.

8. Gracy, "A Preliminary Survey," p. 55.

9. Daniel J. Boorstin, *The Americans: The Democratic Experience*, pp. 274–280.

10. Gracy, "A Preliminary Survey," pp. 71–72; Stephens, "History of Bailey County," pp. 52–53; Willis, "Ghost Towns of the South Plains," pp. 71–72.

11. The exaggeration was not in the numbers of the population but rather the type (the area did support several thousand prairie dogs). Clinton L. Paine, "The History of Lipscomb County" (M.A. thesis, West Texas State Teachers College, 1941), p. 46; Gracy, "A Preliminary Survey," p. 59.

12. Boorstin, *The Americans: The Democratic Experience*, p. 274.

13. Gracy, "A Preliminary Survey," pp. 78–79.

14. Michael T. Kingston, ed., *The Texas Almanac and State Industrial Guide, 1984–1985*, pp. 343–346; U.S. Department of Commerce, Bureau of the Census, *Fourteenth Census of the United States, 1920: Agriculture*, 6: 664–686.

Bibliography

Manuscript Collections

Brunson, Billy Ray. Papers, 1918–1960. Southwest Collection, Texas Tech University, Lubbock.
Contains information on the Texas Land and Development Company.

Conner, Lincoln Guy. Collection. Panhandle-Plains Historical Museum, Canyon, Texas.
Provides information on Conner's activities and other colonization projects.

Double U Company. Records, 1907–1923. Southwest Collection, Texas Tech University, Lubbock.
Extensive collection on the management of the townsite of Post, Texas, and the Post Farm Lands.

Espuela Land and Cattle Company. Records, 1900–1908. Southwest Collection, Texas Tech University, Lubbock.
Set of letterpress books with correspondence relating to the selling of Spur Farm Lands.

Francklyn Land and Cattle Company. Records, 1882–1957. Panhandle-Plains Historical Museum, Canyon.
Contains correspondence concerning the towns of Pampa and White Deer and the work of George Tyng and T. D. Hobart in selling the White Deer Lands.

Gough, L. Collection. Interview file. Panhandle-Plains Historical Museum, Canyon.
Contains the contract of Gough and Witherspoon with the South and West Land Company.

Gracy, Mrs. David C. Papers, 1845–1951. Southwest Collection, Texas Tech University, Lubbock.
A small collection with advertising brochures and photographs.

Keiser, C. O. Papers. Panhandle-Plains Historical Museum, Canyon.

Littlefield, George Washington. Papers, 1860–1919. Eugene C. Barker Texas History Center, University of Texas at Austin.
Some correspondence dealing with the sale of Littlefield Lands and account ledgers showing advertising expenses.

Matador Land and Cattle Company. Records, 1881–1952 and undated. Southwest Collection, Texas Tech University, Lubbock.
Primarily deals with the ranching operations but includes material on the Roaring Springs Townsite Company, 1912–1925.

Naylor, Mrs. John W. Papers. James R. Record Collection of West Texas Pioneers, 1936–1959. Southwest Collection, Texas Tech University, Lubbock.
Contains clippings and typescripts concerning pioneers.

Sanborn, Henry Bradley. Papers, 1896–1950. Panhandle-Plains Historical Museum, Canyon.
The Bravo Ranch correspondence contains extensive material on the selling of the ranch and on colonization practices.

Soash, William Pulver. Papers, 1904–1959. Southwest Collection, Texas Tech University, Lubbock.
Includes correspondence, financial statements, contracts, and advertisements.

Texas Land and Development Company. Records, 1912–1955. Southwest Collection, Texas Tech University, Lubbock.
Contains correspondence, legal materials, and advertising relating to the company's land sales.

XIT Ranch, Texas. Records, 1886–1915. Panhandle-Plains Historical Museum, Canyon.
Extensive records on the operation of the ranch. The annual reports contain information on experimental crops, townsite development, and land colonization plans.

Government Documents

Texas. Agricultural Experimental Station. *A History of Small Grain Crops in Texas: Wheat, Oats, Barley, Rye, 1582–1976.* By Irvin M. Atkins, College Station [1980].

———. *Report of the Director on the Establishment of the New State Stations.* By H. H. Harrington. Austin: Austin Printing Co., 1910.

Texas. Department of Agriculture. *The Panhandle and Llano Estacado of Texas.* By Frederick W. Mally. Bulletin 12. Austin: Von Boeckmann-Jones, 1910.

U.S. Congress. House of Representatives. *Production of Rain by Artillery Firing.* House Report 786. 43d Cong., 1st sess., 1874.

U.S. Congress. Senate. *Experiments in Production of Rainfall.* Senate Executive Document 45. 52d Cong., 1st sess., 1892.

U.S. Department of Agriculture. *Yearbook of Agriculture, 1900.* Washington, D.C., 1901.

————. *Yearbook of Agriculture, 1904.* Washington, D.C., 1905.

————. *Yearbook of Agriculture, 1905.* Washington, D.C., 1906.

————. *Yearbook of Agriculture, 1908.* Washington, D.C., 1909.

————. *Yearbook of Agriculture, 1909.* Washington, D.C., 1910.

————. *Yearbook of Agriculture, 1911.* Washington, D.C., 1912.

U.S. Department of Commerce. Bureau of the Census. *Fourteenth Census of the United States, 1920: Agriculture.* Vol. 6, Part 2. Washington, D.C., 1925.

Books

Bartlett, John Russell. *Personal Narrative of Explorations and Incidents in Texas, New Mexico, California, Sonora, and Chihuahua.* 2 vols. London: George Routledge, 1854.

Beadle, J. H. *The Undeveloped West; or, Five Years in the Territories.* Philadelphia: National Publishing Company, 1873.

Blankenship, Mary A. *The West Is for Us: The Reminiscences of Mary A. Blankenship.* Edited by Seymour V. Connor. Lubbock: West Texas Museum Association, 1958.

Boorstin, Daniel J. *The Americans: The Democratic Experience.* New York: Random House, 1973.

————. *The Americans: The National Experience.* New York: Random House, 1965.

Brockett, L. P. *Our Western Empire: Or the New West beyond the Mississippi.* Philadelphia: Bradley, Garretson, 1881.

Brunson, B. R. *The Texas Land and Development Company: A Panhandle Promotion, 1912–1956.* Austin: University of Texas Press, 1970.

Burnside, Wesley M. *Maynard Dixon: Artist of the West.* Provo, Utah: Brigham Young University Press, 1974.

Connor, Seymour V., ed. *Builders of the Southwest.* Lubbock: Southwest Collection, 1959.

Crosby County Historical Commission. *A History of Crosby County, 1876–1977.* Dallas: Taylor Publishing, 1978.

Eaves, Charles Dudley, and C. A. Hutchinson. *Post City, Texas: C. W. Post's Colonizing Activities in West Texas.* Austin: Texas State Historical Association, 1952.

Elliott, Richard Smith. *Notes Taken in Sixty Years.* St. Louis: R. P. Studley and Company, 1883.

Emmons, David M. *Garden in the Grasslands: Boomer Literature of the Central Great Plains.* Lincoln: University of Nebraska Press, 1971.

Gammel, H. P. N., ed. *The Laws of Texas, 1822–1897.* 10 vols. Austin: Gammel Book Company, 1898.

Gracy, David B. *The Littlefield Lands: Colonization on the Texas Plains, 1912–1920.* Austin: University of Texas Press, 1968.

Graves, Lawrence, ed. *A History of Lubbock.* Lubbock: West Texas Museum Association, 1962.

Gregg, Josiah. *Commerce of the Prairies.* 1844. Reprint. Edited by Max L. Moorhead. Norman: University of Oklahoma Press, 1954.

Green, Donald E. *Land of the Underground Rain: Irrigation on the Texas High Plains, 1910–1970.* Austin: University of Texas Press, 1973.

Gressley, Gene M. *Bankers and Cattlemen.* New York: Knopf, 1966.

Haley, J. Evetts. *Charles Goodnight: Cowman and Plainsman.* Norman: University of Oklahoma Press, 1949.

———. *The XIT Ranch of Texas and the Early Days of the Llano Estacado.* Norman: University of Oklahoma Press, 1953.

Hogarth, Paul. *Artists on Horseback: The Old West in Illustrated Journalism, 1857–1900.* New York: Watson-Guptill, 1972.

Holbrook, Frederick. *The Dead Horseman; or Phantom Riders of Texas.* New York: George Munro, 1876.

Holden, William Curry. *Alkali Trails.* Dallas: Southwest Press, 1930.

Hunt, David C. *Legacy of the West.* Omaha, Nebraska: Center for Western Studies, Joslyn Art Museum, 1982.

Jones, Billy M. *Health-Seekers in the Southwest, 1817–1900.* Norman: University of Oklahoma Press, 1967.

Lewis, Alfred Henry. *The Throwback: A Romance of the Southwest.* New York: Outing Publishing, 1906.

Murrah, David J. *C. C. Slaughter: Rancher, Banker, Baptist.* Austin: University of Texas Press, 1981.

Nichols, Roger L., and Patrick L. Halley. *Stephen Long and American Frontier Exploration.* Newark: University of Delaware Press, 1980.

Overton, Richard C. *Burlington West: A Colonization History of the Burlington Railroad.* Cambridge, Massachusetts: Harvard University Press, 1941.

————. *Gulf to Rockies: The Heritage of the Fort Worth and Denver–Colorado and Southern Railways, 1861–1898.* Austin: University of Texas Press, 1953.

Paxton, Frederic Logan. *The Last American Frontier.* New York: Macmillan, 1910.

Pearce, William M. *The Matador Land and Cattle Company.* Norman: University of Oklahoma Press, 1964.

Pomeroy, Earl. *In Search of the Golden West: The Tourist in Western America.* New York: Knopf, 1957.

Powell, John Wesley. *Report on the Lands of the Arid Region of the United States, with a More Detailed Account of the Lands of Utah.* 1879. Reprint, Boston: Harvard Common Press, 1983.

Rathjen, Frederick W. *The Texas Panhandle Frontier.* Austin: University of Texas Press, 1973.

Reid, Captain Mayne. *The White Chief: A Legend of North Mexico.* New York: Carleton, 1877.

Sheffy, Lester F. *Francklyn Land and Cattle Company.* Austin: University of Texas Press, 1963.

————. *The Life and Times of Timothy Dwight Hobart, 1855–1935.* Canyon, Texas: Panhandle-Plains Historical Society, 1950.

Smith, Henry Nash. *Virgin Land: The American West as Symbol and Myth.* New York: Vintage Books, 1950.

Spikes, Nellie Witt, and Temple Ann Ellis. *Through the Years: A History of Crosby County, Texas.* San Antonio: Naylor, 1952.

Texas Almanac and State Industrial Guide, 1910. Dallas: A. H. Belo, 1910.

Texas Almanac and State Industrial Guide, 1984–1985. Edited by Michael T. Kingston. Dallas: A. H. Belo, 1983.

Tice, John H. *Over the Plains and on the Mountains, or, Kansas and Colorado: Agriculturally, Mineralogically, and Aesthetically Described.* St. Louis: Industrial Age Printing Company, 1872.

Webb, Walter Prescott. *The Great Plains.* Boston: Ginn, 1931.

Wheeler, Keith. *The Chroniclers.* New York: Time-Life Books, 1976.

Articles

Archambeau, E. R. "Early Panhandle Newspapers." *Panhandle-Plains Historical Review* 45 (1972): 46–54.

Athearn, Robert G. "The Great Plains in Historical Perspective." *Montana* 8 (Winter 1958): 13–29.

Baker, Ray Stannard. "The Great Southwest." *Century Magazine,* May–June 1902, pp. 5, 213, 216, 221.

Baker, T. Lindsay. "The White Deer Polish Colony." *Panhandle-Plains Historical Review* 56 (1983): 19–32.

Billingsley, William S. "The FW & DC Railroad: Giving Birth to a Line of Communities in West Texas." *Texas Humanist*, May–June 1983, pp. 16–18.

Black, William M., and Lowell H. Harrison. "C. O. Keiser and the Farmers' Settlement of Randall County." *Panhandle-Plains Historical Review* 43 (1970): 51–71.

Bowden, Martyn J. "The Perception of the Western Interior of the United States, 1800–1870: A Problem in Historical Geosophy." *Proceedings of the Association of American Geographers* 1 (1969): 16–21.

Burgess, Roger A. "Pioneer Quaker Farmers of the South Plains." *Panhandle-Plains Historical Review* 1 (1928): 116–123.

Casey, Don. "The Early History of Shallowater." *Museum Journal* 12 (1970): 99–146.

Connor, Seymour V. "Early Land Speculation in West Texas." *Southwestern Social Science Quarterly* 42 (March 1962): 354–362.

———. "The Founding of Lubbock." In *A History of Lubbock*, edited by Lawrence Graves, pp. 68–97. Lubbock: West Texas Museum Association, 1962.

———. "The New Century." In *A History of Lubbock*, edited by Lawrence Graves, pp. 98–126. Lubbock: West Texas Museum Association, 1962.

Crowell, Chester T. "Six-Shooter Ethics." *The Independent*, 5 December 1912, pp. 1312–1314.

Dillon, Richard H. "Stephen Long's Great American Desert." *Proceedings of the American Philosophical Society* 3 (April 1967): 93–108.

Draper, William R. "Passing of the Texas Cowboy and the Big Ranches." *Overland Monthly*, February 1905, pp. 146–150.

Dreiser, Theodore. "The Railroad and the People: A New Educational Policy Now Operating in the West." *Harper's New Monthly Magazine*, February 1900, pp. 479–484.

Ericson, J. E. "Colonization of the Spur Farm Lands." *West Texas Historical Association Yearbook* 31 (October 1955): 41–53.

Everett, Dianna, and Cathey Kelly. "First, You Work: Germans from Russia to Texas." *Panhandle-Plains Historical Review* 56 (1983): 65–83.

Gates, Paul W. "The Role of the Land Speculator in Western Development." In *Public Lands: Studies in the History of the Public Domain*, edited by Vernon Carstensen, pp. 349–367. Madison: University of Wisconsin Press, 1963.

Gracy, David B. "Arthur P. Duggan and the Early Development of Littlefield." *West Texas Historical Association Yearbook* 44 (October 1968): 38–47.

——. "A Preliminary Survey of Land Colonization in the Panhandle-Plains of Texas." *Museum Journal* 11 (1969): 53–79.

——. "Selling the Future: A Biography of William Pulver Soash." *Panhandle-Plains Historical Review* 50 (1977): 1–75.

Graves, Lawrence. "Economic, Social, and Cultural Developments." In *A History of Lubbock*, edited by idem, pp. 192–234. Lubbock: West Texas Museum Association, 1962.

Green, Donald E. "The Speculator as a Promoter and Developer of Irrigation on the Texas High Plains, 1910–1920." *West Texas Historical Association Yearbook* 46 (1970): 187–197.

Harrington, Mark W. "Farwell's Rainfall Scheme." *American Meteorological Journal* 8 (June 1891): 84–91.

Hauptman, Laurence M. "Mythologizing Westward Expansion: Schoolbooks and the Image of the American Frontier before Turner." *Western Historical Quarterly* 8 (1977): 269–282.

Hayne, Frank H. "Early Days in Parmer County," *West Texas Historical Association Yearbook* 23 (October 1947): 25–29.

Hazen, H. A. "Rain Making." *Scientific American* 65 (October 1982): 277.

Hicks, John D. "The Western-Middle West, 1900–1914." *Agricultural History* 20 (April 1946): 65–76.

Holden, William C. "Immigration and Settlement in West Texas." *West Texas Historical Association Yearbook* 5 (June 1929): 66–86.

Holt, R. D. "Texas Had Hot County Elections." *West Texas Historical Association Yearbook* 24 (October 1948): 3–26.

Jordan, Terry G. "The German Settlement of Texas after 1865." *Southwestern Historical Quarterly* 73 (October 1969): 193–212.

McClain, Meredith, and Judy Harrell. "The Persistence and Change of Ethnicity: A Study of the German-Catholic Community of Nazareth, Texas." *Panhandle-Plains Historical Review* 56 (1983): 141–150.

Marovitz, Sanford E. "Bridging the Continent with Romantic Western Realism." In *The American Literary West*, edited by Richard W. Etulain, pp. 17–28. Manhattan, Kansas: Sunflower Press, 1980.

Mehls, Steven F. "Garden in the Grassland Revisited: Railroad Promotion Efforts and the Settlement of the Texas Plains." *West Texas Historical Association Yearbook* 55 (1984): 47–66.

Nall, Garry L. "The Farmer's Frontier in the Texas Panhandle." *Panhandle-Plains Historical Review* 45 (1972): 1–20.

————. "Panhandle Farming in the 'Golden Era' of American Agriculture." *Panhandle-Plains Historical Review* 46 (1973): 68–93.

Peckham, Howard. "Books and Reading on the Ohio Valley Frontier." *Mississippi Valley Historical Review* 44 (March 1958): 649–663.

Petersen, Peter L. "A New Oslo on the Plains: The Anders L. Mordt Land Company and Norwegian Migration to the Texas Panhandle." *Panhandle-Plains Historical Review* 49 (1976): 25–54.

————. "Patterns in Assimilation: Two German-Lutheran Congregations in the Texas Panhandle." *Panhandle-Plains Historical Review* 56 (1983): 101–113.

Rickard, J. A. "South Plains Land Rushes." *Panhandle-Plains Historical Review* 2 (1929): 98–103.

"Selling Texas Land at Retail: Success of the W. D. Soash Land Company Due to Advertising." *Judicious Advertising and Advertising Experience*, July 1908, pp. 24–28.

Sheffy, Lester F. "The Experimental Stage of Settlement in the Panhandle of Texas." *Panhandle-Plains Historical Review* 3 (1930): 78–103.

Sherman, Caroline B. "The Development of American Rural Fiction." *Agricultural History* 12 (January 1938): 67–76.

Sokolow, Jayme A. "The Demography of a Ranching Frontier: The Texas Panhandle in 1880." *Panhandle-Plains Historical Review* 55 (1982): 73–126.

"Texan Ethics." *The Independent*, 5 December 1912, pp. 1324–1325.

Vigness, David M. "Transportation." In *A History of Lubbock*, edited by Lawrence Graves, pp. 393–416. Lubbock: West Texas Museum Association, 1962.

Walker, Harry S. "Economic Development of Lubbock." In *A History of Lubbock*, edited by Lawrence Graves, pp. 300–340. Lubbock: West Texas Museum Association, 1962.

Weaver, Bobby D. "Father Joseph Reisdorff: Catholic Colonizer of the Plains." *Panhandle-Plains Historical Review* 56 (1983): 127–140.

Newspapers

Amarillo Daily News, 1910–1912.
Amarillo Herald, 1905.
Canyon City News, 1903–1908.
Crosbyton Review, 1909–1916.

Daily Panhandle (Amarillo), 1911.
Dalhart Texan, 1903.
Des Moines (Iowa) *Register and Leader*, 1909–1911.
Fort Worth Star-Telegram, 1913.
Hale County Herald, 1913.
Hereford Brand, 1902–1909.
Lamb County Leader (Littlefield), 1963.
Littlefield News, 1912.
Lubbock Avalanche, 1905–1907.
Plainview Evening Herald, 1914.
Randall County News, 1908–1917.
Reeves County Record, 1911.
The Earth, 1904–1911 (a Santa Fe Railway publication).
The Stayer (Canyon), 1901–1902.
Texas Livestock Journal (Fort Worth), 1887.
West Texas News (Scurry County), 1914.

Land Brochures

Amarillo Chamber of Commerce. *The Land of Promise.* Amarillo: Press of the Panhandle, 1911.
Atchison, Topeka and Santa Fe Railway. *Panhandle and South Plains of Texas.* Chicago: Henry O. Sheppard Company, [1911].
Brown, Pat, comp. *Land Promotion in Crosby County.* N.p., n.d.
Canyon City, Texas. Printed for Thompson Hardware Co. Dallas: Southwestern Folder Co., n.d. In Land Company Brochures File, Panhandle-Plains Historical Museum, Canyon.
Dillard-Powell Land Company. *Lubbock, Lubbock County: The Best Cheap Lands in the Southwest for Diversified Farming.* Lubbock: Dillard-Powell, [1908]. In Ratliff Papers, Southwest Collection, Texas Tech University, Lubbock.
Farwell Development Company. *Farwell, Texas.* Chicago, n.d. In Land Company Brochures File, Panhandle-Plains Historical Museum, Canyon.
Fort Worth and Denver City Railway. *Facts about Texas with Special Information Concerning the Panhandle.* New York: American Bank Note Company, n.d.
Gibbs, G. G. *Homes in the Panhandle of Texas.* San Antonio: San Antonio Printing, [1906].
Gumley, James Thomas, comp. *Information Concerning Shafter Lake in Andrews County.* N.p., n.d.
Hereford Commercial Club. *Camera Chat from Hereford on the Plains in the Panhandle of Texas.* Hereford: Hereford Brand, n.d.

In Land Company Brochures File, Panhandle-Plains Historical Museum, Canyon.

Hobart, T. D. *White Deer Lands in the Panhandle of Texas.* Pampa, n.d.

Lubbock Commercial Club. *Short but Forceful Story of the Plains and Lubbock County.* Lubbock: Avalanche Printing Company, [1909].

Lubbock: The Railroad Center of the Plains. Lubbock: Bledsoe and Price, [1910]. In Bledsoe Papers, Southwest Collection, Texas Tech University, Lubbock.

McDonald, D. L. *Where Crops Never Fail.* Kansas City, Missouri: Union Bank Note Company, n.d.

Missouri, Kansas and Texas Railway. *Texas: Empire State of the Southwest.* N.p., 1911.

Missouri Pacific Railway Company. Statistics and Information Concerning the State of Texas. St. Louis: Woodward and Tiernan Printing, 1889.

Moody Land Company. *Moody Farm Lands.* Kansas City, Missouri: Moody Land Company, [1908].

Olton Townsite Company. *We Wish to Tell You of the New County Seat 'Olton.'* Kansas City, Missouri: Schooley Stationary, [1908]. In Soash Papers, Southwest Collection, Texas Tech University, Lubbock.

Progressive Panhandle—Armstrong, Carson and Potter Counties. Amarillo: Russell and Cockrell, n.d.

Rawlings-Knapp Realty Company. *Littlefield Lands: The Best Farm Lands.* Kansas City, Missouri: Rawlings-Knapp Realty Company, n.d.

Reservation Lands: 500,000 Acres Offered for Sale as Farm Homes. N.p., n.d. In Land Company Brochures File, Panhandle-Plains Historical Museum, Canyon.

Shallow Water Land Company. *Information about Hale County, Texas: The Shallow Water Country.* Plainview, n.d. In Land Company Brochures File, Panhandle-Plains Historical Museum, Canyon.

Seagraves, C. L. *Farmers Make Good in the Panhandle and South Plains of Texas.* Chicago: Rogers and Smith Printers, [1911].

Short and Williams Real Estate Company. *Land in the Panhandle of Texas.* Kansas City, Missouri: Burd and Fletcher Printing, 1906.

Silverton Commercial Club. *Briscoe County: Growth and Development of the Great Plains of Texas.* Silverton: Enterprise Print, [1910].

South and West Land Company. *The Last of the Great Prairie Farming Lands.* Chicago, [1906].

W. P. Soash Land Company. *The Big Springs Country of Texas.* Waterloo, Iowa: Stewart-Simmons Press, [1909].

Spur Farm Lands. Stamford: Stamford Tribune Print, [1908].

Stock Farms and Small Ranch Tracts in the Famous Spur Ranch of Northern Texas. Kansas City, Missouri: Union Bank Note Company, n.d.

Stratton Land Company. *Invest a Few Dollars in a New Town.* Wichita, Kansas: Stratton Land Company, n.d.

Texas Commercial Secretaries Association. *Texas Opportunities.* Fort Worth: Texas Commercial Secretaries Association, 1910.

Texas and Pacific Railway. *West Texas: The Land of Opportunities.* St. Louis: Burton and Skinner, [1907].

Willis, John H. *Facts from the Farmers and Stock Raisers of the Panhandle of Texas.* N.p., n.d. In Land Company Brochures File, Panhandle-Plains Historical Museum, Canyon.

Young Men's Business Club of Canadian. *Canadian the Beautiful.* Wichita, Kansas: McCormick-Armstrong Press, n.d. In Land Company Brochures File, Panhandle-Plains Historical Museum, Canyon.

Unpublished Works

Black, William M. "C. O. Keiser's Economic Activities in Randall County, Texas." M.A. thesis, West Texas State College, Canyon, 1960.

Buckner, Kyle M. "History of Brownfield, Texas." M.A. thesis, Texas Technological College, Lubbock, 1943.

Burgess, Roger A. "The History of Crosby County." M.A. thesis, University of Texas, Austin, 1927.

Douglas, Louva Myrtis. "The History of the Agricultural Fairs of Texas." M.A. thesis, University of Texas, Austin, 1943.

Flanagin, Charles P. "The Origins of Nazareth, Texas." M.A. thesis, West Texas State Teachers College, Canyon, 1948.

Kutzleb, Charles Robert. "Rain Follows the Plow: The History of an Idea." Ph.D. diss., University of Colorado, Boulder, 1968.

Lowe, Ida Marie Williams. "The Role of the Railroads in the Settlement of the Texas Panhandle." M.A. thesis, West Texas State College, Canyon, 1962.

Lynch, Dudley Morton. "Belle of the Prairie Press: A History of *The Hereford Brand:* Sixty-Five Years of Newspapering on the

High Plains of Texas. Seminar paper, University of Texas, Austin, 1966.

Martin, Robert Leslie. "The City Moves West: Economic and Industrial Growth of the Southern Llano Estacado." Ph.D. diss., University of Oklahoma, Norman, 1959.

Murrah, David. "From Ranching to Dry Farming." Paper presented at Sam Blair Lecture Series, South Plains College, 28 October 1983, Levelland.

Nall, Garry Lynn. "Agricultural History of the Texas Panhandle, 1880–1965." Ph.D. diss., University of Oklahoma, Norman, 1972.

Oppe, Hubert Wilhelm. "Umbarger: Its History and People: A Monograph on a German Settlement in the Texas Panhandle." Canyon, June 1964. Mimeographed.

Paine, Clinton L. "The History of Lipscomb County." M.A. thesis, West Texas State Teachers College, Canyon, 1941.

Patrick, Marvin Alton. "A Survey of Land Colonization Companies in Texas." M.B.A. thesis, University of Texas, Austin, 1925.

Plank, Arnold C. "Desert versus Garden: The Role of Western Images in the Settlement of Kansas." M.A. thesis, Kansas State University, Manhattan, 1962.

Stephens, Thelma W. "History of Bailey County." M.A. thesis, Texas Technological College, Lubbock, 1939.

Willis, Roysten E. "Ghost Towns of the South Plains." M.A. thesis, Texas Technological College, Lubbock, 1941.

Wyman, Laura Lynn. "The Quanah, Acme and Pacific Railway." M.A. thesis, Midwestern University, Wichita Falls, Texas, 1967.

Interviews

Abernathy, Mollie D. and Monroe G. Interview by Ike Connor. Lubbock, Texas, 3 and 4 June 1956. Southwest Collection, Texas Tech University, Lubbock.

Carpenter, Lois Bassett. Interview by Pat Brown. Crosbyton, Texas, 25 November 1983. Southwest Collection, Texas Tech University, Lubbock.

Jones, Clifford B. Interview by David B. Gracy. Lubbock, Texas, 28 February and 27 March 1968. Southwest Collection, Texas Tech University, Lubbock.

Index

9 780292 742239